Design Is Storytelling

Ellen Lupton

COOPER HEWITT

PUBLISHED BY
Cooper Hewitt, Smithsonian Design Museum
2 East 91st Street
New York, NY 10128
USA

cooperhewitt.org

DISTRIBUTION (UNITED STATES) BY
ARTBOOK | D.A.P.
75 Broad Street, Suite 630
New York, NY 10004
USA
artbook.com

DISTRIBUTION (WORLDWIDE) BY
Thames & Hudson UK
181A High Hilborn
London WC1V 7QX
UK
thamesandhudson.com

DIRECTOR OF CROSS-PLATFORM PUBLISHING: Pamela Horn
CROSS-PLATFORM PUBLISHING ASSOCIATE: Matthew Kennedy
PRINTER: CG Graphics
BOOK DESIGN: Ellen Lupton and Brooke Thyng
COVER DESIGN: Jason Gottlieb
COVER ILLUSTRATIONS: Jason Gottlieb with Morcos Key
and PostTypography

TYPEFACES: National and Tiempos, designed by Kris Sowersby,
Klim Type; VTC Supermarket Sale, designed by Vigilante
Typeface Corporation

INTERIOR TEXT: Flo matte 80#

2019 / 10 9 8 7 6 5

Printed in China

Library of Congress Cataloging-in-Publication Data

Names: Lupton, Ellen, author.
Title: Design is storytelling / Ellen Lupton.
Description: New York, NY : Cooper Hewitt, Smithsonian Design
Museum, [2017]
| Includes index. | "This book explores connections between
storytelling and design. It examines the psychology of visual
communication from a narrative point of view."—Publisher's
description.
Identifiers: LCCN 2017036709 | ISBN 9781942303190 (pbk.)
Subjects: LCSH: Design—Human factors. | Design—
Psychological aspects. |
Storytelling in art. | Visual communication—Psychological
aspects. |
Creative thinking.
Classification: LCC NK1520 .L867 2017 | DDC 745.4—dc23
LC record available at https://lccn.loc.gov/2017036709

ISBN 978-1-942303-19-0

 Smithsonian Design Museum

Contents

[Curtain is closed.
Stage is dark.]

Overture

Foreword

Caroline Baumann, Director
Cooper Hewitt, Smithsonian Design Museum

Once upon a time, museums were staid palaces of culture. These formal and forbidding places sought to safeguard the treasures of civilization. Today's museums are more open and participatory. People come here to look, learn, make, and converse.

At Cooper Hewitt, Smithsonian Design Museum, storytelling is part of everything we do. We tell stories about the lives of designers, the process of design, the power of technology, and the evolution of materials. We tell stories about how communities create change and how designers have built their own profession. Every exhibition, event, and web entry has a dynamic narrative arc.

Cooper Hewitt's visitors devise their own stories from the artifacts and ideas they find here. Every museum visit is a unique path through a sensory world. Those paths have peaks of intensity and points of rest. A professional designer or a college student will have a different museum experience—and a different story to tell— than a third-grader or an international tourist.

Cooper Hewitt publishes original works of scholarship across all media, from exhibition catalogues and monographs devoted to design minds to e-books and even coloring books. Each publication has a point of view about how and why design is practiced. This book, *Design Is Storytelling*, is a new contribution to the field of design education. Ellen Lupton, Cooper Hewitt's longtime curator of contemporary design, has gathered here a fascinating range of insights about the narrative impact of design. This fun and practical book will be useful to designers, educators, students, and clients alike—and to anyone interested in using design to inspire action and stir emotion. Enjoy!

Acknowledgments

Ellen Lupton, Senior Curator of Contemporary Design
Cooper Hewitt, Smithsonian Design Museum

I first approached my colleagues at Cooper Hewitt with an idea for a book about design and storytelling in September, 2015. I am so delighted and thankful that the concept was enthusiastically supported by Caroline Baumann, Director, and Cara McCarty, Curatorial Director. It has been a privilege to work on this book with their support and expert guidance.

I never would have finished creating this book without the energy and drive of Pamela Horn, Cooper Hewitt's Director of Cross-Platform Publishing. She pushed me to keep moving when the task felt impossible, and she constantly brought me new sources and directions to explore. She supported the creative process in every way and made this book a personal priority. Matthew Kennedy is an editorial partner with exquisite judgment and wit; working with him is always fun and productive.

Over the past decade, the courses I have taught at Maryland Institute College of Art (MICA) in Baltimore have revolved around experience and communication. Design is no longer focused on static objects and images. Design is a time-based, interactive enterprise. I am grateful to all my students and colleagues at MICA for demonstrating the power of stories and inspiring me with their creative work. I owe special thanks to Marcus Civin, John Dornberger, Brockett Horne, Gwynne Keathley, Jennifer Cole Phillips, and my many graduate and undergraduate students.

It has been my privilege to be a student myself in the MA in Writing program at Johns Hopkins University. It is here that I came to study the theory and mechanics of narrative, and it is here that I began to explore the overlaps between design practice and storytelling. I am grateful for everything I have learned from the faculty at Hopkins, especially from William Black, Mark Farrington, Karen Houppert, and Jeannie Venasco.

Many artists, illustrators, and designers shared their work for this book. I thank each of them for their talent and generosity. However, no single artist contributed more than my dear friend and long-time collaborator Jennifer Tobias. This book is truly our joint effort, a labor of love that filled many weekends with sketching, talking, and musing. I'm also grateful to my friend and teaching colleague Jason Gottlieb for bringing so much care and creativity to the cover design.

Much thanks goes to my friends and family for their patience and interest. I am grateful to my parents (Mary Jane Lupton, Ken Baldwin, William Lupton, and Lauren Carter), my children (Jay Lupton Miller and Ruby Jane Miller), my sister (Julia Reinhard Lupton), my brilliant husband (Abbott Miller), my friends Edward and Claudia, and all the Miller sisters.

Illustration by Adrian Tomine

Inciting Incidents

I first heard the statement "Design is problem solving" when I was an art student at The Cooper Union in New York City. This was the early 1980s—long before the arrival of Photoshop, digital fonts, or the Internet. We were taught that in order to solve visual problems, designers should apply simple forms in a rational manner. The signage system used in New York City's subway was—and is—a brilliant work of problem solving. To create it, Massimo Vignelli and Bob Noorda deployed sans serif type and bright dots of color to unify a network of deteriorating stations. The system, implemented in 1970 after years of research, is easy to understand and efficient to maintain. Problem solved, four decades and counting.

The MTA's signage system tells you more, however, than where to find the A train. When the signs first appeared, those crisp white letters and sharp dots of color annnounced a new language of rational communication. The signs didn't just solve a problem; they embodied ideas and principles. They celebrated the subway's transition from a collection of competing subway lines to a government-owned public authority. They conveyed values about order, reliability, and civic life.

As a student, I felt that problem solving didn't account for everything I wanted to know about design practice. Problem solving wasn't enough. What about beauty, feeling, and sensation? What about humor, conflict, and interpretation? Ever since those student days, I've been asking these questions in my work as a writer and curator. Fascinated by critical theory, I have written about relationships between writing and typography. As a professor at Maryland Institute College of Art (MICA), I have explored experience design, multisensory design, and the psychology of perception. As a curator at Cooper Hewitt, Smithsonian Design Museum, I've looked at how

PROBLEM SOLVING

Brooklyn Bridge City Hall Station
4 5 6 J Z

STORYTELLING

designers have approached feminism, the body, and the user. I marvel at Cooper Hewitt's inclusive collection, which includes everything from Vignelli's abstract map of the New York City subway system to a birdcage shaped like a neo-Gothic cottage. The museum was founded in 1895 as a resource for working artists and designers, including students attending The Cooper Union, the museum's original home. Today, Cooper Hewitt, Smithsonian Design Museum addresses all levels of design education, from kindergarten to grad school.

A subway is more than a rational system. It is a place where people fall asleep, fall in love, get drunk, get lost, and sometimes take their lives. Trains rumble, platforms murmur, and ads hawk everything from underpants to wrinkle cream. In 2008, Yves Béhar designed a line of free condoms (distributed by the city's health department) inspired by New York's subway signs. Applied to condom packaging, the subway's colorful dots represent a city where people move about and freely mingle, a place of love and danger. Béhar practices human-centered design, a methodology that combines rational problem solving with emotional storytelling.

This book explores connections between storytelling and design. Stories depict action and stimulate curiosity. A story can be shorter than a limerick or as long as an epic poem. Design uses form, color, materials, language, and systems thinking to transform the meaning of everything from transit signs and web apps to shampoo bottles and emergency shelters. Design embodies values and illustrates ideas. It delights, surprises, and urges us to action. Whether creating an interactive product or a data-rich publication, designers invite people to enter a scene and explore what's there—to touch, wander, move, and perform.

Design Is Storytelling examines the psychology of visual communication from a narrative point of view. Human beings actively seek and create patterns as we navigate the world— and we feel intrigued, stimulated, and sometimes frustrated when patterns break. Storytelling can help products and communications hook the imagination of users and invite actions and behaviors.

A young woman approached me recently after a lecture in Beirut, Lebanon, eager to discuss creative practice. "What excites me about design," she said, "is the potential to transfer information into someone else's mind." Stories do that, too. Stories travel from person to person and place to place. A well-made sentence moves ideas from the head of a writer to the head of a reader. That's how Steven Pinker talks about writing in his wonderful guide *The Sense of Style*. Good writing communicates more than information, however. Effective storytellers convey emotion, feeling, and personality. They bring characters and settings to life. Exchanging energy—not just transferring data and facts—occurs whenever a product is used, or an image is seen, or a game is played. That energy comes from the dynamic, world-making relationship between creators and audiences, between makers and users.

Design Is Storytelling is a playbook for creative action. The tools and concepts presented here address today's dynamic, user-focused design practices. Throughout the book, readers will discover ways to use graphs, diagrams, writing, and other methods of invention and analysis.

Design Is Storytelling unfolds in three main acts. Act I, "Action," explores the patterns that underlie nearly every story, from the narrative arc to the hero's journey. Designers can apply these patterns to users' relationships with products and services. The process of unboxing a gadget, opening a bank account, or visiting a library follows a dramatic arc with highs and lows, anticipation and suspense. Design is an art of thinking ahead and predicting possible futures. Scenario planning and design fiction encompass a range of tools and techniques for imagining unknown situations, questioning the status quo, and plotting possible futures.

Act II, "Emotion," looks at how design plays with our feelings, moods, and associations. Co-creation helps designers build empathy with users and create solutions that enhance life. No one is happy all the time. A user's emotional journey can include lows as well as highs, hitting points of annoyance and anger as well as satisfaction.

Act III, "Sensation," focuses on perception and cognition. Stories hinge on action, and so, too, does human perception. Concepts such as the gaze, Gestalt principles, and affordances reveal that perception is a dynamic process of creating order and meaning. Research in behavioral economics shows that small design cues can influence decision making. Perception is active and transformative. The people who see, touch, and use our work participate in its realization. Color and form are gateways to multisensory design. Design can guide people in a certain direction, but users will each take their own paths.

The book wraps up with tools for evaluating projects. Tips for writing will help designers convey clear and active stories. A project generator for students and teachers is a table of mix-and-match, do-it-yourself design challenges to try in the classroom or at home. Finally, a storytelling checklist asks a series of questions about the design process. Does your project depict action? Does your project deliver a call to action to users? Have you built empathy with potenital users? Will your project engage viewers in active, creative looking? Have you used design elements to invite action from users?

This is a book about design processes and how to talk about them. Designers use stories to stir emotions and quell uncertainty, to illustrate facts and sway opinions. The process of using an app or planning a trip builds over time, supported along the way with sounds, sights, and physical feedback. Roadblocks and obstacles mar the experience and slow us down (dead batteries, rejected credit cards, or a senseless onslaught of pop-up windows). Each scene in these everyday dramas can be pleasurable or cumbersome, depending on how the experience has been planned.

I hope you will enjoy reading this book, which has been designed for use alongside a designer's active work process. The book is full of playful pictures, which tell their own stories alongside the written ones. I couldn't have created this book without support and inspiration from my colleagues at Cooper Hewitt, Smithsonian Design Museum, and my students and collaborators at MICA.

Designers today produce more than logos and cereal boxes; they create situations that stimulate the mind and body over time.

Act 1 | Action

Illustration by Ellen Lupton

ACT 1

Action

At a conference in New Orleans, a young designer asked me what I was working on. He looked gravely concerned when I told him I was writing a book about storytelling. "Have you heard about the mantle of bullshit?" No, I hadn't.

"Stefan Sagmeister," he explained, "gave an interview saying that storytelling is bullshit. You should see it."

In the interview, Sagmeister denounces a designer who creates roller coasters for theme parks and calls himself a storyteller. According to Sagmeister, storytelling is a "mantle of bullshit" that designers use to load up their work with glamour and prestige. A roller coaster designer doesn't tell stories—he designs roller coasters, and that should be interesting enough on its own.

Yet roller coasters do share a pattern with many stories. The ride starts out on level ground and builds toward a climax. As the cart climbs slowly up the track, it stores energy that will be released in a whooshing drop after the passengers reach the highest point. The energy released by the roller coaster is not only physical but emotional, heard in the ecstatic screams of riders.

Roller coaster designers work to amplify the emotional intensity of the ride, drawing out suspense toward the zenith. In his book *Sonic Boom*, Joel Beckerman writes about a roller coaster designer who inserted a silent pause just before the apex. The unexpected quiet makes riders worry. Is something wrong? Did the machine break? Is something terrible about to happen?

Filmmakers generate suspense with similar techniques, pausing the action before the villain jumps out of the closet. The following pages explore some of the patterns that underlie stories, including the rising and falling energy of the narrative arc and the circular return of the hero's journey.

Illustration by Grant Snider for the *New York Times Book Review*

Designers sometimes think of a building, chair, or poster as a static artifact. Yet we experience each of these things over time. A hospital or airport is a sequence of physical spaces (entry halls, receiving zones, passageways, and seating areas). The rooms in a building change from open to compressed, light to dark, warm to cool, soft to hard, to support different uses. Some activities are quick and intense, while others are slow and relaxed. Architecture isn't "frozen music" because it isn't frozen. Time never stands still.

A poster or an illustration is temporal, too. Eyes wander across its surface, darting from detail to detail to build a whole picture, focusing on some areas and leaving others in the background. A book compresses time and space between two covers. A book has a fixed sequence of pages, yet users can enter—and exit—from any point they choose.

In a novel or movie, the order of events doesn't always match the order in which the audience encounters them. The dastardly deed in a murder mystery often occurs early in the story. Someone has been murdered but we don't know why. (Later we will learn that Bob killed Aunt Mary in order to inherit her rent-controlled apartment.) To write a mystery, the author has to work out the underlying structure (sometimes called the "plot") and then reveal that structure bit by bit (the "story"). The story entices readers with clues and false leads. By the end, the author has shone light into the dark corners of the plot, bringing its secret architecture into view.

Designers plan structures, too. The client's brief for a building or website explains what functions the project will fulfill. A shoe store might need retail space, office space, a stockroom, and a loading dock. A website for the same store might need a product database, e-commerce tools, user accounts, and FAQs. Architects and designers plan the layout of these physical and virtual places as well as plan different paths people could take through them. UX designers use diagrams and site maps to chart the structure of an app or website, and they create user flows to predict potential journeys.

One of the most famous tales in Western literature is *Oedipus Rex*. An oracle tells the king of Thebes that his own son will eventually kill him, so the king wounds his newborn child (Oedipus) and abandons him outdoors to die. (What could possibly go wrong?) A kindly shepherd rescues the baby, who grows up to slay the king in a fit of road rage on his way to destroy the evil Sphinx, a monster blocking the entrance to the city of Thebes. Oedipus defeats the Sphinx and is declared king—an honor that involves marrying the queen. Alas, the queen is Oedipus's mother. When the royal couple discover what they have done, she hangs herself, and he pokes out his eyes. End of story.

Aristotle used *Oedipus Rex* as a universal template for storytelling. The essence of drama, he wrote, is action. Characters, scenery, and moral lessons exist for just one purpose: to underscore the main action of the story. In an effective narrative, the main action must attain sufficient "magnitude," culminating in dastardly deeds or profound discoveries. The chicken can't just cross the road; she needs a compelling reason to do so (reunite with egg; serve paternity papers to rooster), and she needs to overcome obstacles along the way (roadkill, left-turning cyclist, zealous traffic cop).

Stories ask questions and delay the answers. The main action of any dramatic tale can be phrased as a question ("Will Oedipus escape his fate?" "Will the chicken deep-fry the rooster for his crimes?"). Finding out the answer yields a satisfying ending that completes the action and makes the story whole.

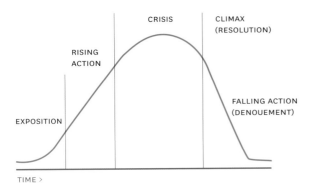

CRISIS

CLIMAX (RESOLUTION)

RISING ACTION

FALLING ACTION (DENOUEMENT)

EXPOSITION

TIME >

LOOKS LIKE A ROLLER COASTER In the words of Jack Hart, "A true narrative arc sweeps forward across time, pushing ahead with constant motion. It looks like a wave about to break, a pregnant package of stored energy." Illustration adapted from Jack Hart, *Storycraft: The Complete Guide to Writing Narrative Nonfiction* (Chicago: University of Chicago Press, 2011).

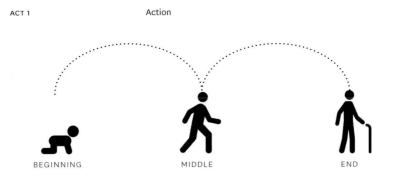

BEGINNING   MIDDLE   END

The Sphinx blocking the gates of Thebes asks every traveler a riddle. She destroys anyone who cannot answer. Here's the riddle: "What walks on four legs in the morning, two legs during the day, and three legs at night?" The answer, replies Oedipus, is a human being. He crawls as a baby, walks upright as an adult, and carries a cane in old age. The riddle of the Sphinx divides human life into three parts: beginning, middle, end.

Action drives stories, and it also drives the design process. Design makes things happen in the world. The word "action" is at the heart of "interaction." "Design" is a verb as well as a noun. At the start of the creative process, designers ask what a product or service can do for people—and what *people* can do with *it*. What actions does a product enable? A calendar doesn't just list events. It's a tool for mapping one of life's most precious resources. A photo album isn't just a place to store pictures. It's a way to edit and share personal histories.

Like an absorbing story, a well-designed product, place, or image unfolds over time. It helps us create memories and forge connections. It contains characters, goals, conflicts, and vivid, sensory settings. In a crowd-funding pitch for a theft-resistant bicycle, dramatic camera angles and suspenseful music turn the bike and its riders into crime-fighting heroes. In a shop selling sultry dresses and eccentric housewares, soft light and the scent of nutmeg convey spicy domesticity. Every pie chart, retail space, food package, and hospital room expresses values through language and light, color and shape. We touch design with our minds and bodies. Sound, texture, taste, and smell prompt our actions and fuel our memories.

TOOL

Narrative Arc

In 1863, the German playwright and novelist Gustav Freytag created the **narrative arc**. He divided dramatic works into five parts: exposition, rising action, climax, falling action, and conclusion or denouement. Freytag's up-and-down pattern is often visualized as a pyramid, placing the climax at the highest point in the action. This useful diagram is also known as Freytag's pyramid or Freytag's triangle.

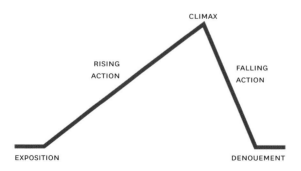

NARRATIVE ARC— THREE LITTLE PIGS

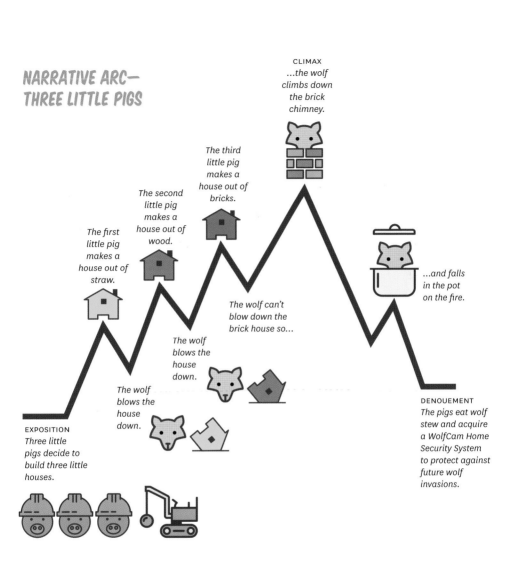

CLIMAX
...the wolf climbs down the brick chimney.

The third little pig makes a house out of bricks.

The second little pig makes a house out of wood.

The first little pig makes a house out of straw.

...and falls in the pot on the fire.

The wolf can't blow down the brick house so...

The wolf blows the house down.

EXPOSITION
Three little pigs decide to build three little houses.

The wolf blows the house down.

DENOUEMENT
The pigs eat wolf stew and acquire a WolfCam Home Security System to protect against future wolf invasions.

THREE LITTLE PIGS Each scene in a story is a smaller arc or pyramid that contributes to the larger shape of the narrative. In the story of "The Three Little Pigs," the first two pigs build flimsy houses with straw and sticks, and the last pig builds a sturdy house with bricks. Each of the houses brings us closer to the final showdown, when the wolf climbs down the chimney of the brick house and falls into the soup pot. The pigs eat the wolf for dinner and live happily ever after. Wolf illustration by Chanut is Industries.

READ MORE Donna Lichaw, *The User's Journey: Storymapping Products That People Love* (Brooklyn, NY: Rosenfeld Media, 2016).

Narrative Arc

UPS AND DOWNS Surging from high to low and back again gives stories their satisfying sense of completion. Complex narratives contain stories within stories and conflicts within conflicts.

A narrative begins with an inciting incident or a call to action. Cinderella gets her call to action when the king invites every maiden in the land to the royal ball. If Cinderella went straight to the ball, met the prince, and got married, there would be no story. If the three little pigs all built safe, sturdy houses with affordable mortgage payments in a wolf-free community, there would be no conflict and no problems to solve.

A full-blown novel or film breaks down into dozens of smaller scenes and beats. Nearly every shot in a movie is driven by a goal or intention. In a well-crafted sentence, the verb pulls the subject forward. In a product design, every user action— from logging in to sharing content—is a smaller scene in a larger narrative.

Design decisions support users' goals and intentions. Does a certain color, font, or texture inspire emotions or trigger a response? Does a product's visual and verbal language underscore its use? Are the required steps clear and engaging?

Many experiences that people enjoy conform to the pattern of beginning/middle/end. Eating a falafel sandwich starts with anticipation. The appetite is stoked by the sight and smell of fried chickpeas swaddled in bread, sauce, and vegetables. The experience peaks as the process of eating finally begins. At last, a heavy gut says, "Stop! It's over!" Having sex follows a similar path, reaching a brilliant high point before drifting into mellow satisfaction. Untying a beautifully wrapped gift or popping open a bag of chips signals the beginning of a story. The rustle of paper and the smell of salty snacks fuel our desire.

The design of anything from step-by-step instructions to an enticing headline or an onscreen menu can initiate a dramatic arc that moves from low to high, desire to satisfaction. A gentle beep or a reassuring click tells users an action is complete. Designers use the rising and falling arc of narrative to emphasize large and small actions.

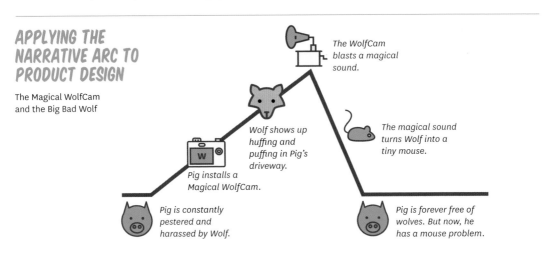

APPLYING THE NARRATIVE ARC TO PRODUCT DESIGN

The Magical WolfCam and the Big Bad Wolf

The WolfCam blasts a magical sound.

Wolf shows up huffing and puffing in Pig's driveway.

The magical sound turns Wolf into a tiny mouse.

Pig installs a Magical WolfCam.

Pig is constantly pestered and harassed by Wolf.

Pig is forever free of wolves. But now, he has a mouse problem.

FOOD AND SEX—
PLEASURE CYCLES

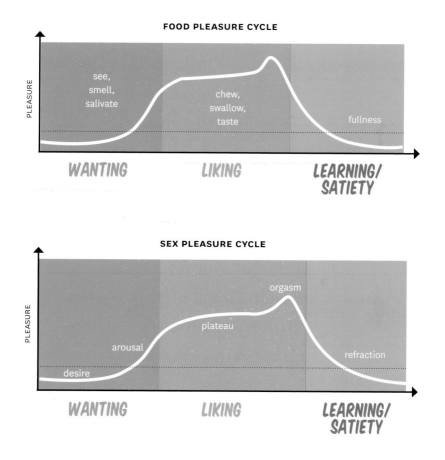

PLEASURE SCIENCE Brain activity rises, peaks, and falls during a good meal or a sexual encounter. This pattern resembles the rising and falling action in a story. Charts adapted from Morten L. Kringelbach, Alan Stein, and Tim J. Hartevelt, "The functional neuroanatomy of food pleasure cycles," *Physiology and Behavior* 106 (2012): 307-316; and J.R. Georgiadis and M. L. Kringelbach, "The human sexual response cycle: Brain imaging evidence linking sex to other pleasures," *Progress in Neurobiology* 98 (2012): 49-81.

TOOL

Hero's Journey

The circular pattern of the **hero's journey**
occurs in tales across history, from Homer's
Odyssey to *Star Wars* and *Mad Max: Fury
Road.* A call to adventure draws the hero
away from ordinary life. Aided by a mentor, a
sidekick, or a wise guide, the hero crosses the
threshold into the unknown. In *The Wizard
of Oz*, Dorothy searches for a better existence
in the Emerald City. She finds a magic pair
of shoes, attracts a band of helpers, battles
villains, and ultimately finds what she is
looking for back in the place she started. She
goes home to Kansas with new knowledge.

ROUND AND ROUND Joseph Campbell traced the hero's journey
in his famous book *The Hero with a Thousand Faces*, published
in 1949. He applied the concept of the circular path to
numerous examples from world literature. The hero's journey
typically includes a call to adventure, the aid of a helper, and a
descent into a strange new place—often a "green world" such
as an Edenic garden or Emerald City. Illustration by
Chris Fodge.

ORDINARY
WORLD

CALL TO
ADVENTURE

RETURN WITH
ELIXIR

REFUSAL OF
THE CALL

RESURRECTION

ORDINARY
WORLD

MEETING
THE MENTOR

THE ROAD
BACK

CROSSING
THE THRESHOLD

SPECIAL
WORLD

REWARD

TESTS, ALLIES,
ENEMIES

SEIZING THE
SWORD

APPROACH

ORDEAL, DEATH,
AND REBIRTH

Hero's Journey

ENTER THE LABYRINTH With its affordable meals and daycare services, an IKEA store can keep an entire family busy for hours. Some shoppers love the store so much, they come and spend the night in the bedding department.

Yet despite the big blue store's popular products and remarkable amenities, sometimes an IKEA store feels like a maze, designed to trap and confuse hapless shoppers. A hero on a quest for a desk chair must endure a gauntlet of living room vignettes and kitchen scenarios before finding the office section. An IKEA store is not, however, a maze. It's a labyrinth! A *maze* is a puzzle with hidden turns and dead ends where a wanderer could be lost forever. A *labyrinth* is a fixed path, designed to carry a person along a controlled journey with a clear beginning and end. Labyrinths have existed in Catholic churches since the Middle Ages. They were invented for meditative purposes, allowing a worshipper to walk in prayer for a great distance within a small space. A labyrinth is designed to be disorienting, but because it provides a single route, the wanderer will never be truly lost.

Architect Alan Penn explains that an IKEA store establishes a guided route that visitors are more or less compelled to follow. After passing through the portal of the Entrance Lobby, shoppers ascend into the Showroom, where miniature rooms entice them to imagine their own homes transformed into compact paradises of modern efficiency. The hero takes notes along the way, collecting locations for items that must be retrieved downstairs in the Warehouse Area. Before reaching the Warehouse, however, the hero must pass through the vast Market Hall, stocked with ready-to-grab kitchen wares and bed linens. At this point, shoppers find themselves suddenly free to put away their tiny pencils and fill their carts with merchandise in a fit of grab-and-go consumption.

MAZE Puzzle designed to confuse

LABYRINTH Long, guided path

Ordinary World

THE IKEA LABYRINTH

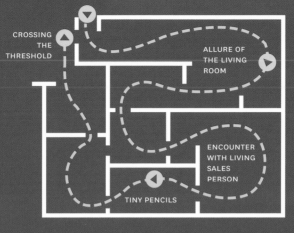

CROSSING THE THRESHOLD

ALLURE OF THE LIVING ROOM

ENCOUNTER WITH LIVING SALES PERSON

TINY PENCILS

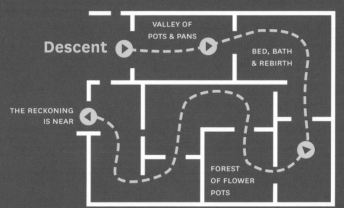

Descent

VALLEY OF POTS & PANS

BED, BATH & REBIRTH

THE RECKONING IS NEAR

FOREST OF FLOWER POTS

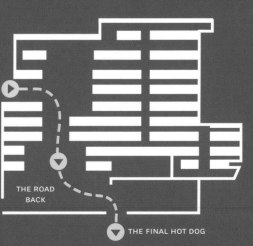

Belly of the Warehouse

THE ROAD BACK

THE FINAL HOT DOG

Illustration by Ruby Miller

Hero's Journey

GUIDED PATH A visit to a mall or supermarket can be as a harrowing as the road to Oz. Shopping malls are common triggers for anxiety and panic attacks. Even a normal visit can leave a traveler burdened with credit card debt and dubious treasures.

Going to the mall with companions can ease the trauma, unless one is escorted by a bored boyfriend or a pack of angry toddlers instead of a tin man and a cowardly lion.

In the typical American grocery store, fresh food occupies the edge of the store (meat, dairy, produce, bakery, and prepared foods). Food activist Michael Pollan warns the intrepid traveler to stay at the green edge of the store as much as possible. However, to find a package of quinoa or gummy bears, you will have to venture deep inside what grocery executives call the *center store*, stocked with shelf after shelf of brightly colored cans, bags, and boxes.

Exhibition designers also grapple with guiding visitors along a path. In their pioneering work "Fundamentals of Exhibition Design" (1939), Bauhaus veterans Herbert Bayer and Laszlo Moholy-Nagy explain how to create a guided path through a series of galleries. At the time, museums typically were designed as boxy rooms connected by symmetrical doorways. Although plans designed with this traditional central axis seem calm and orderly, Bayer and Moholy-Nagy found—surprisingly—that halls with asymmetrical openings actually move people along in a more controlled way.

Bayer and Moholy-Nagy advocated a multisensory, multimedia approach to exhibition design, employing graphic arrows, phonographic recordings, and mechanized "moving carpets" to move people through space. Today, curators and exhibition designers continue to use signage, lighting, sound, barriers, and distinctive landmarks to compel visitors to follow a linear narrative. At the end of the labyrinth, they will often find a gift shop.

ODYSSEY OF THE SUPERMARKET The healthier food in a supermarket is concentrated around the edges of the store, while processed foods dominate the center. Many fresh foods require refrigeration and access to kitchen areas, which makes it economical for stores to keep those goods in the outer zone. Illustration by Jennifer Tobias.

READ MORE Herbert Bayer and Laszlo Moholy-Nagy, "Fundamentals of Exhibition Design," The New York Public Library Digital Collections, 1939-12-1940-01; Alan Penn, "The Complexity of the Elementary Interface: Shopping Space," University College London; Michael Pollan, *Food Rules: An Eater's Manual* (New York: Penguin Books, 2009); Michael Powell, "All Lost in the Supermarket," *Limn*, Issue Four: Food Infrastructures (May 2014). http://limn.it/all-lost-in-the-supermarket/; accessed June 12, 2016.

EXHIBITION JOURNEY

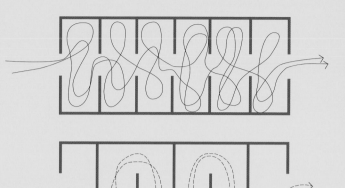

SYMMETRY VS. ASYMMETRY Classical museum buildings feature halls that lead into each other with symmetrically placed doorways. Although the floor plan looks orderly, visitors don't know where to go first when they enter a new gallery. Asymmetrical openings allow curators to control the narrative.

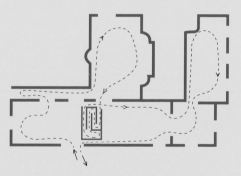

ODD-SHAPED ROOMS Exhibition designers use barriers and wall graphics to move visitors through an assortment of odd rooms.

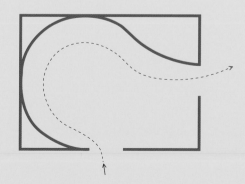

ONE PATH, ONE STORY Curators and designers can sometimes produce a unified experience by creating a simple and unambigous path. This may not be the most satisfying experience for visitors.

FAST FOOD DRAMA SCHOOL

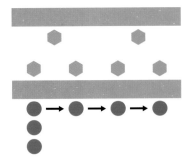

CHIPOTLE

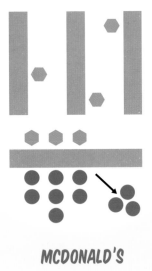

MCDONALD'S

MAPPING A SERVICE Any product or service has a plot. Designers ask, "What is the desired action? How does the user complete the action?" People go to a restaurant not just for the food, but for a satisfying experience. At Chipotle, guests participate in a drama. The process is active and transparent. At McDonald's, customers wait in line to order and then wait in line again to pick up food. Food is prepared in the background by servers who don't communicate directly with customers. A palpable sense of passive waiting clouds the experience.

RESTAURANT AS THEATER Designing a fast-food business involves more than figuring out what food to serve. It requires architecture, interiors, logos, packaging, menus, social media strategies, and ways to move customers in and out of the store.

A visit to a fast-food restaurant is an adventure in design and branding. The intrepid hero seeking sustenance waits in line, orders a dish, and pays the bill. Sound, materials, and graphics add atmosphere and build dramatic tension. The store layout supplies a consistent pattern of action.

At the burrito-bowl purveyor Chipotle, customers participate in constructing the meal. As they select beans, cheese, and four kinds of salsa to fill their cardboard vessels, they take part in an active drama. Price lists and calorie counts build emotional tension. The process is transparent rather than hidden, allowing them to witness the food they are about to eat while absorbing the sound, sight, and smell of meat sizzling in the background. By the time they reach the register, their food is ready to go. Chips, drinks, and guacamole complicate the final reckoning.

For contrast, imagine a trip to McDonald's. Customers wait in line, tell the cashier what they want, pay their bill, and then wait again. They may not be sure *where* to wait—there's no clearly designated spot, just a huddled mass of other customers with hunger in their hearts and receipts in their hands. They never interact with the people who prepare their food—these employees are busy in the middle ground or hidden away in a mechanized netherworld. This disconnected process neither empowers customers to serve themselves nor involves them in a satisfying action. The McDonald's user flow is convenient for McDonald's but not especially pleasing to patrons, while the flow at Chipotle is fun and engaging.

Dozens of restaurants in the "fast casual" market segment—from the salad chain Chopt to the Korean diner Korilla—have embraced a transparent and engaging process similar to Chipotle's. Some restaurants have concierges to help customers through the process, keeping the line moving while keeping the process interesting. Meanwhile, as these more personal fast-food experiences become popular, customers are also seeking radically impersonal services—choosing to order online and pick up food or have it delivered with as little human contact as possible. Services like Seamless and Deliveroo cater to this ATM model of food service, while delivery-only restaurants have become another business model.

Every brand tells a story about a business, product, service, or place. Chipotle's Mexican-themed interiors underscore the adventure of ordering food. Room dividers and trash kiosks made from corrugated metal suggest low-cost construction in a Mexican village. In many Chipotle outlets, loud music, hard surfaces, and narrow stools encourage people to eat quickly or carry their food out the door. Whereas soft chairs and WiFi in a coffee shop encourage longer visits—and a second cup of joe—Chipotle has little to gain from slowing down the pace.

Where must we go, we who wander this wasteland, in search of our better selves? *MAD MAX: FURY ROAD*, GEORGE MILLER, DIRECTOR

TOOL

Storyboard

Telling stories with a sequence of images is an invaluable skill not only for filmmakers, comic book artists, and graphic novelists, but for any designer working with time and interactivity. The purpose of a **storyboard** is to explain action with a concise series of pictures. To construct a storyboard, designers plan the arc of a narrative and decide how to summarize the story in a limited number of frames. How does the story begin and end? What is the setting? Where are the story's points of greatest intensity? Do characters or other objects walk, run, or roll into the scene—or do they magically appear in a blast of confetti? Storyboards for animations or videos indicate camera movements in addition to plot points.

Illustration by Hayelin Choi

Sonia Delaunay arrives.

Zoom in.

Zoom in.

Zoom out.

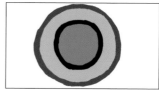

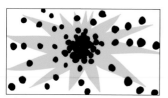

Frida Kahlo appears.

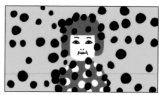

Cut.

Wham!

Yayoi Kusama appears.

Storyboard

DESIGNING A SATISFYING STORY There is a famous joke that is funny because it refuses to be funny: "Why did the chicken cross the road? *To get to the other side.*" We expect a punch line, but all we get is a mundane activity lacking any compelling motivation or outcome.

In a satisyfing narrative, the main action is signficant or noteworthy, yielding a transformation or shift in the world of the story. The character can change, or she can change the people or events around her. By solving an important problem, the character sees herself in a new way.

A satisfying story includes conflict and suspense. Questions create uncertainty, making readers curious. The story is the process of answering the question and resolving the uncertainty. If the answer comes too easily, the story is dull. Stories thrive on obstacles, delays, and moments of revelation. A story is a winding path, not a straight and efficient line.

Like stories, many jokes function by flipping our understanding of an initial situation. The set up puts a picture in our minds; the punch line shatters that picture. Woody Allen recounts this joke in his movie *Annie Hall*: "A guy walks into a psychiatrist's office and says, hey doc, my brother's crazy! He thinks he's a chicken. Then the doc says, why don't you turn him in? Then the guy says, I would but I need the eggs." The punch line changes the premise implied in the set up.

Storyboards are tools for planning the transformative action of a story. In a few simple frames, a good storyboard expresses a progression from beginning to middle to end. It conveys an intriguing path and a signifcant change. It indicates necessary details and the point of view of each scene (near or far, first person or third person). Learning to tell a story in six frames is a good way to master the essential elements of narrative form.

READ MORE Uri Shulevitz, *Writing with Pictures: How to Write and Illustrate Children's Books* (New York: Watson-Guptill, 1985).

Ingredients of a Story

ARC The action has a beginning, middle, and end.

CHANGE The action transforms a character or situation.

THEME The action conveys a greater purpose or meaning.

COHERENCE The action builds on concrete, relevant details.

PLAUSIBILTY The action is believable, following its own rules.

Here's the beginning of a story: "Chicken steps into the road, and a truck approaches from the distance." What happens next?

1. MAGIC CHICKEN In this version of the story, a magic balloon lifts Chicken to safety. The magic balloon is a cheap way to solve the story's central problem. Using it requires no skill or ingenuity from our hero (or from the storyteller). It's also implausible. An inflated blob of latex wouldn't move quickly enough to save Chicken from a speeding truck. Even fantasy tales should mesh with our basic expectations about physics.

2. DEAD CHICKEN The truck hits Chicken. End of story. This turn of events—dramatic as it is—fails to quench our thirst for meaning. The dead bird is not only a defeated protagonist but also a passive one. She hasn't completed the story's action, and she hasn't controlled her own destiny. Furthermore, she is carrying around a useless and redundant fish. This "red herring" adds neither action nor meaning to the narrative.

3. TOUGH CHICKEN This is the best version of the story. Here, Chicken is an active character, shaping the course of events. At the beginning, she appears to be a solitary, oblivious bird adrift in a dangerous world. When she halts traffic and guides the baby chicks to safety, she becomes a player on a bigger stage and contributes to the social good. The action yields a greater purpose or theme, altering our initial assumptions.

Illustrations by Jennifer Tobias

HOW DOES THE CHICKEN CROSS THE ROAD?

There are three ways this story could end. Which one feels more satisfying and complete?

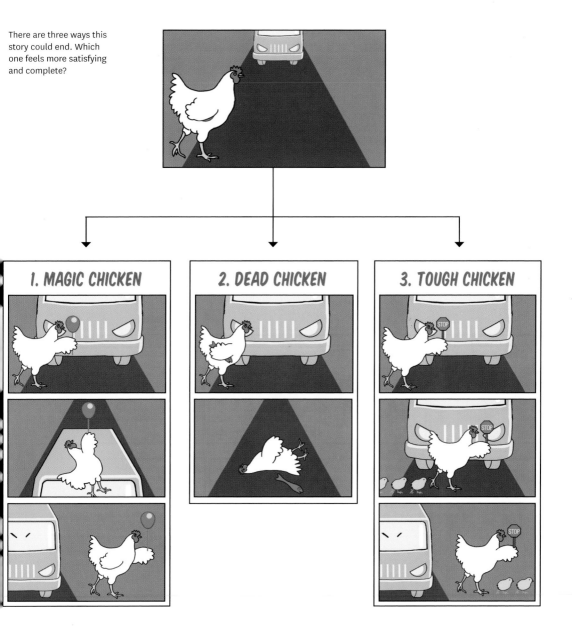

Storyboard

THINKING WITH STORYBOARDS Designers use storyboards to communicate their ideas to clients and collaborators. Designers also use narrative illustrations to think through a problem, sketch ideas, and empathize with users as they confront everyday challenges.

Storyboards are a crucial tool in the human-centered practice of industrial designer Mengyan Li. She starts her design process by searching for "problems and opportunities" that involve users in personal situations. To brainstorm product concepts for cyclists, Li imagined situations where people get frustrated trying to bring their bikes on a car or bus trip. Li says, "Storytelling is the most effective tool to make audiences enjoy a presentation, make them patient and curious to accept an idea, help them better understand an instruction, and keep them awake in lectures. People love cute stuff." Her storyboards convey the emotional quality of a user's experience.

In addition to creating illustrations of people interacting with a product in a physical context, designers produce storyboards to plan the actions that take place on a digital screen when a product is being used. The storyboards created by user experience designers range from simple, black-and-white wireframes to fully developed flats, which represent a product's visual language in rich detail. Wireframes or flats often follow the sequence of a user's journey, from an "inciting incident" or call to action (the event that triggers engaging with the product) through a series of steps required to successfully achieve a goal or complete an action.

PLOT, CHARACTER, AND SETTING These poignant and appealing storyboards depict frustrating situations for cyclists. Each story brings us into a scene infused with real emotional consequences. A cyclist going to work can't get on the bus because there isn't enough room for her bike. Three friends enjoying a ride in the country meet another friend in a car. The driver wants to take everyone to the lake—but the car's trunk is too small for all the bikes. Illustrations by Mengyan Li.

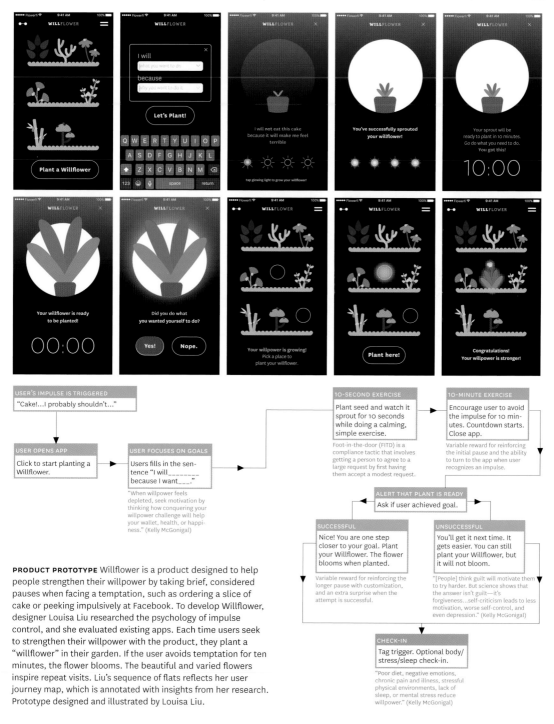

USER'S IMPULSE IS TRIGGERED
"Cake!...I probably shouldn't..."

10-SECOND EXERCISE
Plant seed and watch it sprout for 10 seconds while doing a calming, simple exercise.

Foot-in-the-door (FITD) is a compliance tactic that involves getting a person to agree to a large request by first having them accept a modest request.

10-MINUTE EXERCISE
Encourage user to avoid the impulse for 10 minutes. Countdown starts. Close app.

Variable reward for reinforcing the initial pause and the ability to turn to the app when user recognizes an impulse.

USER OPENS APP
Click to start planting a Willflower.

USER FOCUSES ON GOALS
Users fills in the sentence "I will_____ because I want___."

"When willpower feels depleted, seek motivation by thinking how conquering your willpower challenge will help your wallet, health, or happiness." (Kelly McGonigal)

ALERT THAT PLANT IS READY
Ask if user achieved goal.

SUCCESSFUL
Nice! You are one step closer to your goal. Plant your Willflower. The flower blooms when planted.

Variable reward for reinforcing the longer pause with customization, and an extra surprise when the attempt is successful.

UNSUCCESSFUL
You'll get it next time. It gets easier. You can still plant your Willflower, but it will not bloom.

"[People] think guilt will motivate them to try harder. But science shows that the answer isn't guilt—it's forgiveness...self-criticism leads to less motivation, worse self-control, and even depression." (Kelly McGonigal)

CHECK-IN
Tag trigger. Optional body/stress/sleep check-in.

"Poor diet, negative emotions, chronic pain and illness, stressful physical environments, lack of sleep, or mental stress reduce willpower." (Kelly McGonigal)

PRODUCT PROTOTYPE Willflower is a product designed to help people strengthen their willpower by taking brief, considered pauses when facing a temptation, such as ordering a slice of cake or peeking impulsively at Facebook. To develop Willflower, designer Louisa Liu researched the psychology of impulse control, and she evaluated existing apps. Each time users seek to strengthen their willpower with the product, they plant a "willflower" in their garden. If the user avoids temptation for ten minutes, the flower blooms. The beautiful and varied flowers inspire repeat visits. Liu's sequence of flats reflects her user journey map, which is annotated with insights from her research. Prototype designed and illustrated by Louisa Liu.

TOOL
Rule of Threes

Three is a magic number. Groups of three appear in life, literature, and product marketing: three wishes, three pigs, three smartphone plans. A simple task has three easy steps, and a story has three basic parts: beginning, middle, end. Writers and comedians use the **rule of threes** to create lists whose last item is unexpected, as in "life, liberty, and the pursuit of happiness" or "sex, drugs, and rock 'n roll." In each of these phrases, the last element breaks the pattern set in motion by the first two. Designers use three-part structures to construct stories and interactions that surprise and satisfy.

THREE-PANEL STORIES This illustrated subway campaign features happy encounters with Casper, a mail-order mattress. Each story is built around a familiar phrase, such as "breakfast in bed" or "face your demons." The story unfolds in three simple drawings. The final frame reveals a twist or surprise that makes the story funny. Campaign designed by Red Antler. Illustrations by Tomi Um.

Rule of Threes

ONE, TWO, THREE Next time you see a three-step guide to downloading an app or activating a product, look closer to find out if the number really matches up with the process. The seductive power of three often masks a longer set of tasks.

Breaking down a process into three basic steps tells users that an action is easy to learn and quick to complete: "Ready, set, go." A three-step sequence—annotated with big numbers or graphic icons—depicts a narrative arc that ramps up quickly and yields a satisfying conclusion. Four steps can also feel compact and accessible, but more than four suggests a process that demands a bigger commitment.

Consider a recipe for scrambled eggs. If you start by explaining how to crack an egg, and gradually build up to finding a pan and turning on the stove, you will soon be telling a very long tale indeed. If you make a few assumptions, however, about what people might reasonably know about kitchens and eggs, you could easily create a three-step algorithm for the novice egg-scrambler.

It's not so easy to bake a soufflé or build a space ship. Designers sometimes merge smaller tasks into bigger ones to put users at ease. That's okay, as long as you don't cause confusion about what the task requires.

In addition to depicting a basic story arc, threes can be powerful memory aids. Writers know this when they construct a punchy list that ends with a bang ("the butcher, the baker, the candlestick maker"). Information designers break down phone numbers and credit card numbers into chunks of three or four to make them easier to remember. Many screenplays are structured in three acts, and many restaurant meals have three courses. Apps and websites often offer users three choices at key points of engagement, such as "Enroll," "Log In," and "Ask Me Later."

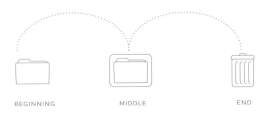

BEGINNING   MIDDLE   END

GRAVEYARD

BLACK HOLE

DESKTOP DRAMA The simple interaction of deleting computer files employs animation and sound to grant the user magical feelings of power and dominion in a world of fictional folders and virtual trashcans. Describing an action in three steps makes it follow a simple story arc. Designer Andrew Peters imagined alternative endings to the familiar story of tossing desktop files into a trashcan.

SHREDDER

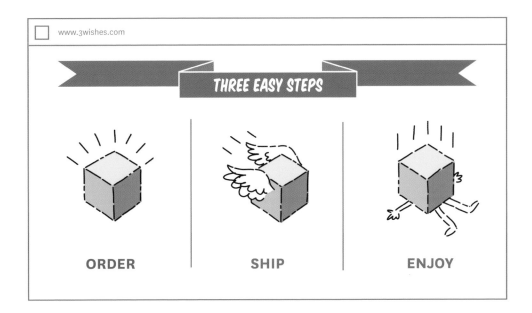

www.3wishes.com

THREE EASY STEPS

ORDER   SHIP   ENJOY

THREE LITTLE PIGS
CONSTRUCTION INC

STRAW

STICKS

BRICK

EAT

PAY

LOVE

THREE STEPS, THREE CHOICES It takes courage to buy stuff. Depicting a process in three steps makes it look painless, and many digital forms offer just three options. According to some research studies, people who are faced with too many choices may be less inclined to make any decision at all. "The Tyranny of Choice," *The Economist*, December 16, 2010, http://www. economist.com/node/17723028; accessed July 29, 2017.

CHOICE ARCHITECTURE Designing the conditions in which individuals make decisions is called *choice architecture*. Users tend to choose defaults, such as pre-checked boxes. Thus designers and other choice architects should carefully consider what defaults to present. Richard Thaler, Cass R. Sunstein, and Sean Pratt, *Nudge: Improving Decisions about Health, Wealth, and Happiness* (London: Penguin Books, 2009).

TOOL

Scenario Planning

Whether the future is next year or next century, it will be different from what anyone expects. **Scenario planning** is a tool for telling stories about the future. Businesses, communities, and organizations use scenario planning to think creatively about the future rather than staying stuck in the present. Scenario planners stress that a scenario is not a prediction. No one knows what will actually happen in the future. We do know that the conditions of today (the present) did result from decisions that were made in the past. Likewise, the decisions we make now will most certainly affect the future—we just don't know how.

THE CONE OF PLAUSIBILITY

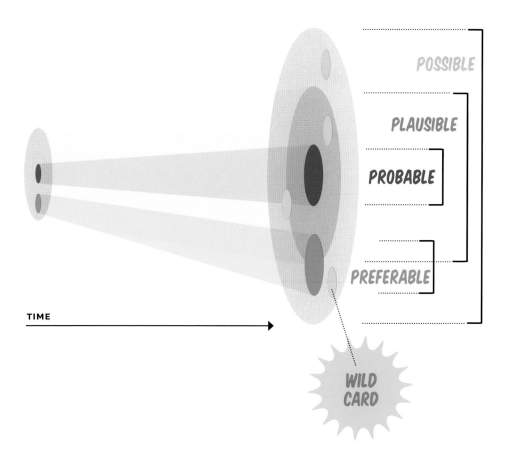

POSSIBLE

PLAUSIBLE

PROBABLE

PREFERABLE

TIME

WILD CARD

CONE OF PLAUSIBILITY The cone of plausibility looks like a funnel. The narrowest point is the present. The cone widens as it looks toward the future, where circumstances are less known. A scenario is considered "plausible" if it proceeds in a logical manner from known trends or developments. Adapted from Trevor Hancock and Clement Bezold, "Possible Futures, Preferable Futures," *The Healthcare Forum Journal* (March 1994): 23–29. Illustration by Jennifer Tobias.

Scenario Planning

CONE OF PLAUSIBILITY Scenario planners use the *cone of plausibility* to diagram future developments based on past or present trends. Achieving preferred (rather than probable) outcomes requires rethinking old habits and pushing past the status quo.

Military strategist Charles W. Taylor invented the cone of plausibility in 1988. As a member of the armed forces who studied military readiness, Taylor feared several developments that could cause government support for the military to decline in the future. In one scenario, U.S. policy could become more isolationist, causing military spending to drop. Alternatively, military growth would be stimulated by an increase in peace-keeping missions.

Imagine Tipsy Cola, a major soft drink company exploring the future of bottled beverages. Tipsy's sales have declined as consumers seek healthier and more sustainable choices. It is *probable* that Tipsy's sales will keep declining and eventually stabilize. It is *preferable* that the company will grow and thrive by addressing the changing demands of consumers and the environment.

Wild-card scenarios include the future discovery that sugary beverages make kids smarter, or the passage of future laws holding soft drink companies responsible for recycling their own bottles and cans. Reviewing these scenarios helps the product team generate wild new ideas, such as pill-shaped water enhancers, resuable packaging, and edible soda bottles.

A cone of plausibility can also look to the past as a source for current trends. A town planner might study how cities functioned before cars became popular. A product designer might explore how a new app or gadget displaced older solutions to a similar problem.

Blurble is an imaginary digital widget. Blurble's CEO believes this clever product will dominate the market forever, but the design team thinks the future is a dark and stormy place full of dangers for Blurble. Today, it's hard to imagine life before Blurble, but people once roamed the Earth without it. Future threats include the rise of Blurble sharing or a global crackdown on Blurble's reckless endangerment of consumer privacy.

Blurble's scenario planners look at particular decisions they could make in the present and then explore the possible outcome of these decisions in relation to one or more variables. For example, making Blurble open-source could yield creative contributions from the community and help Blurble thrive. Wild-card catastrophes could include a massive recall of exploding Blurbles or the invasive spread of driverless, paperless, self-cleaning Blurble clones.

READ MORE Charles W. Taylor, *Alternative World Scenarios for a New Order of Nations* (Carlisle Barracks, PA: Strategic Studies Institute, 1993).

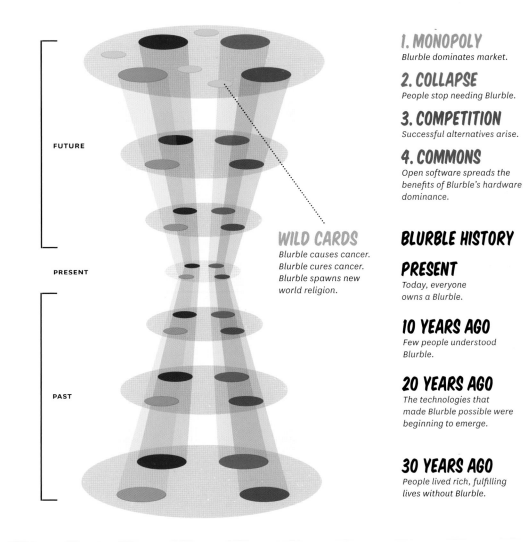

BLURBLE—
FOUR PLAUSIBLE
FUTURES

FUTURE

PRESENT

PAST

1. MONOPOLY
Blurble dominates market.

2. COLLAPSE
People stop needing Blurble.

3. COMPETITION
Successful alternatives arise.

4. COMMONS
Open software spreads the benefits of Blurble's hardware dominance.

WILD CARDS
Blurble causes cancer. Blurble cures cancer. Blurble spawns new world religion.

BLURBLE HISTORY

PRESENT
Today, everyone owns a Blurble.

10 YEARS AGO
Few people understood Blurble.

20 YEARS AGO
The technologies that made Blurble possible were beginning to emerge.

30 YEARS AGO
People lived rich, fulfilling lives without Blurble.

Illustration by Jennifer Tobias

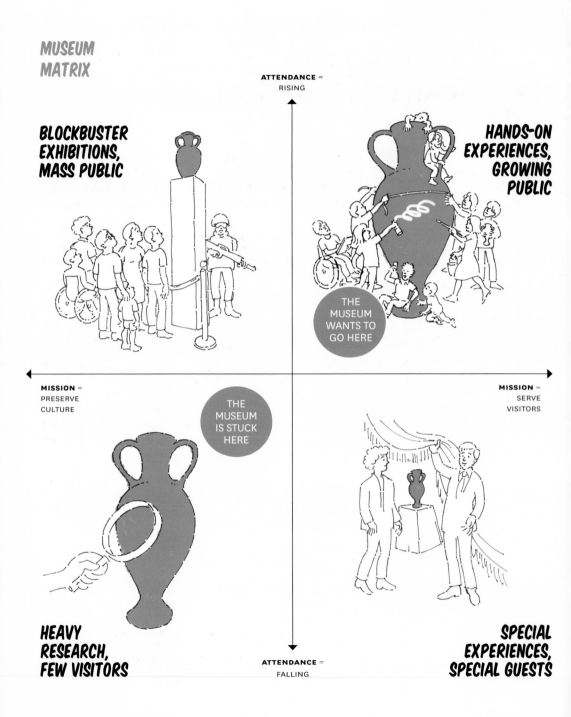

MUSEUM MATRIX

ATTENDANCE = RISING

BLOCKBUSTER EXHIBITIONS, MASS PUBLIC

HANDS-ON EXPERIENCES, GROWING PUBLIC

THE MUSEUM WANTS TO GO HERE

MISSION = PRESERVE CULTURE

MISSION = SERVE VISITORS

THE MUSEUM IS STUCK HERE

HEAVY RESEARCH, FEW VISITORS

SPECIAL EXPERIENCES, SPECIAL GUESTS

ATTENDANCE = FALLING

SCENARIO MATRIX A *scenario matrix* is a tool for mapping choices on an x/y axis. The grid generates four quadrants that help decision makers think about how two variables interact.

Matrix diagrams are commonly used in scenario planning. Each quadrant in the four-square matrix supports a different scenario. Often, one quadrant represents the status quo or "business as usual." The other quadrants suggest new directions that could be explored and developed.

To create a scenario matrix, make a list of forces affecting your product, organization, or community. Strategist Jay Ogilvy calls these forces *critical uncertainties*. They might include changes in social structures, consumer preferences, income levels, or government spending and regulations. From your list, choose two forces to map onto the four-square matrix. Think about what would happen to your product or organizaiton if each of these quadrants became dominant. Give each quadrant a compelling name.

The Metro Museum of Regional Art is located in a postindustrial town. Public funding has dropped, and so has attendance. Worries range from practical matters ("How can we afford to stay open?") to existential questions ("Why are we here?"). The Metro Museum collects objects related to local history, but few people visit the museum's dimly lit galleries lined with traditional glass cases. The town doesn't attract many tourists. How can the Metro Museum better serve the immediate community?

The planning team creates a matrix with two axes: Attendance and Mission. Each quadrant inspires a different story about the museum's future. A simple phrase assigned to each scenario makes the stories easy to remember and easy to talk about. After discussing the scenarios, the museum decides to actively create hands-on experiences for new audiences. Instead of curators doing their research in hidden labs, citizen experts will become part of the process. The Metro Museum can now begin designing exhibitions and outreach campaigns that will help the institution achieve this future.

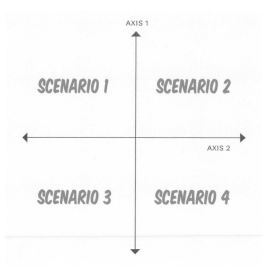

AXIS 1

SCENARIO 1   SCENARIO 2

AXIS 2

SCENARIO 3   SCENARIO 4

READ MORE Jay Ogilvy, "Scenario Planning and Strategic Forecasting," Forbes, January 8, 2015, http://www.forbes.com/sites/stratfor/2015/01/08/scenario-planning-and-strategic-forecasting/#62786e6b7b22; accessed January 9, 2017. Illustrations by Jennifer Tobias.

TOOL

Design Fiction

Like novelists, many designers have a gift for observing current society and technology. **Design fiction** employs speculative products and prototypes to anticipate future trends or propose visionary solutions to vexing problems. When science fiction writers conjure imaginary worlds, the settings they envision can be utopian or dystopian. Likewise, some design fictions depict gleaming futures filled with tech-enabled products, while others imagine darker outcomes. Speculative design amplifies current social and technological developments. Such projects often look ahead to reflect upon the present world.

THE FUTURE OF UNDERWEAR

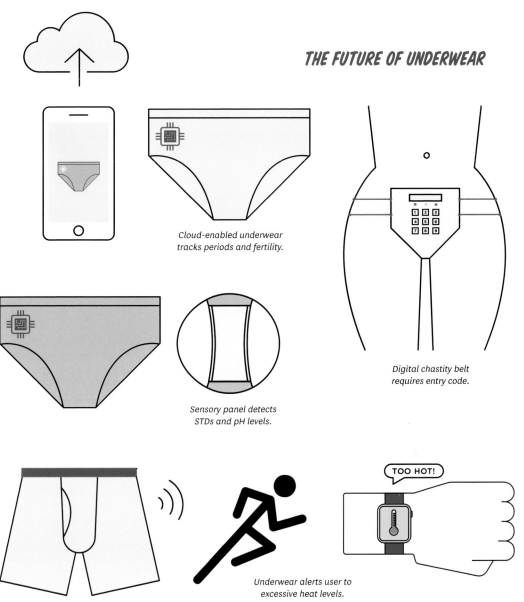

Cloud-enabled underwear
tracks periods and fertility.

Sensory panel detects
STDs and pH levels.

Digital chastity belt
requires entry code.

TOO HOT!

Underwear alerts user to
excessive heat levels.

FICTIONAL UNDERPANTS A team of designers gathered to think about the future of underwear. Tech-enhanced underwear could improve health and well-being. Technology could also lead to new modes of control and surveillance. Concepts by Claire Moore and Miles Holenstein. Project concept and illustrations by Claire Moore.

Design Fiction

FUTURE STUFF Whether expressed via rough sketches or elaborately realized imaginary worlds, design fictions offer a rich arena for visualizing future life and picturing both the dangers and promise of technology.

Gary Shteyngart's novel *Super Sad True Love Story*, published in 2010, takes place in an exaggerated rendition of New York City in the early twenty-first century. This super-sad future includes stark income inequality, privacy-killing social media, and a dysfunctional U.S. political system controlled by global corporations. Shteyngart successfully predicted future events because he was a close observer of the present. Similarly, the British television series *Black Mirror* (created by Charlie Brooker, 2011) presents narratives about the future that amplify aspects of today's social media; each episode visualizes imaginary digital interfaces that are eerily real and profoundly disturbing.

Many design projects are conceived as speculative proposals for the future. Exotic concept cars and lavishly art-directed videos for tech companies celebrate the wonders of growth and innovation. Other veins of design fiction are more critical. Anthony Dunne and Fiona Raby have developed a practice they call *conceptual design*. They created this practice with graduate students as a form of research that envisions alternatives to present existence. Dunne and Raby's fictional artifacts—from a plush-toy atomic mushroom cloud to an emotionally needy robot—hint at "a parallel world of everyday philosophical products."

Conceptual design refuses to deliver market-ready products or enticing images of a glittering future. Like science fiction in novels and films, design fiction often asks where today's excesses, inequalities, and errors might be taking us.

Several designers and art/design collectives have created decks of cards for inventing fictional products. These decks use simple variables (analogous to the "suits" in standard playing cards) to generate random design prompts. The Thing from the Future, created by Stuart Candy and Jeff Watson, is a game that helps teams and individuals build stories about the future. Each story consists of an object, a mood, a setting, and a narrative arc. Shuffling the deck yields endless combinations. Players can purchase physical cards or print DIY decks from an open-source PDF. The game can be played with groups of students or other participants as a co-creation activity.

The Thing from the Future is a storytelling machine. Turning the design process backwards, it uses signals from a distant world to inspire new thinking. Candy calls this process *reverse archaeology*. The results can be humorous or provocative as well as practical. The game stimulates serious conversations about social and environmental sustainability.

Once designers step away from industrial production and the marketplace, we enter the realm of the unreal, the fictional, or what we prefer to think of as conceptual design—design about ideas. ANTHONY DUNNE AND FIONA RABY

SOME THINGS FROM THE FUTURE

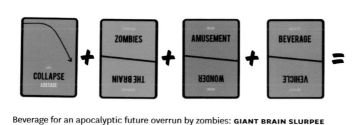

Beverage for an apocalyptic future overrun by zombies: **GIANT BRAIN SLURPEE**

Totalitarian device using eye-tracking software to control what we see: **EYE PAD**

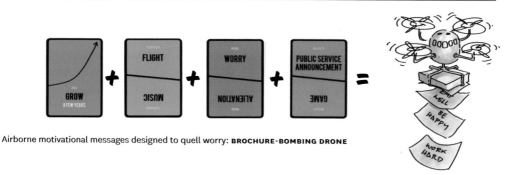

Airborne motivational messages designed to quell worry: **BROCHURE-BOMBING DRONE**

THE THING FROM THE FUTURE The original deck has four suits: Object, Terrain, Mood, and Arc. The Arc suggests what kind of future to imagine ("growth," "collapse"). The Terrain card determines the context ("learning," "zombies"). The Mood card sets the emotional tenor ("worry," "amusement"). The Object card suggests what product to design ("beverage," "device"). The Thing from the Future recalls Oblique Strategies, a card deck created by Brian Eno and Peter Schmidt in 1975. Game designed by Stuart Candy and Jeff Watson. Illustrations by Jennifer Tobias.

READ MORE Gary Shteyngart, *Super Sad True Love Story* (New York: Random House, 2010); Anthony Dunne and Fiona Raby, *Speculative Everything: Design, Fiction, and Social Dreaming* (Cambridge, MA: MIT Press, 2013); Stuart Candy, "Dreaming Together," *The Sceptical Futuryst*, November 22, 2015, https://futuryst.blogspot.com/2015/11/dreaming-together_81.html; accessed January 8, 2017.

FORCED CONNECTIONS: UNDERWEAR FROM THE FUTURE

DISPOSABLE

The word "disposable" triggered ideas for paper underwear. Then, the designer sought out sustainable alternatives. What would a caveman wear? Concepts by Erica Holeman.

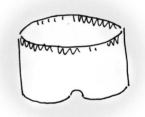

RELIGIOUS

Ideas for "religious" underwear began with using scripture as ornament and inspiration. Then, the idea of "illumination" led to underpants that glow in the dark. Concepts by Erica Holeman.

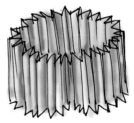

MECHANICAL

What if underwear could change in response to emotional distress? These pink panic pants wiggle to provoke laughter. The blue pants open up to let in extra air or tighten up to hug the body. Concepts by Ninad Kale.

Design Fiction

FORCED CONNECTIONS Clashing ideas merge into new symbols, creating metaphors, puns, and potent symbols. Clever products also arise from combining disparate functions, materials, or processes.

Getting together with a group of designers is a productive way to generate concepts. Most designers have participated in group brainstorming sessions. A moderator collects everyone's ideas during a short, intense meeting; negative comments are not allowed. The sticky note— a star player in most brainstorming sessions— has become an icon for design thinking.

Brainstorming with sticky notes is not the only way to generate ideas in a group. Try slowing down and giving participants some simple prompts and enticing art supplies. (A tray of cookies helps, too.) Designer Claire Moore led a workshop exploring the future of underwear. To jumpstart the process, she gave each designer an attribute to apply to the basic notion of undergarments. Attributes

included "disposable," "mechanical," "religious," and "skeumorphic." Inspired by these prompts, designers came up with concepts ranging from underwear printed with Bible passages to paper boxer shorts and panic-control panties.

The initial prompt pushed each designer to come up with surprising new forms and functions for familiar undergarments. This process works with individuals as well as with groups. To get started, make a list of adjectives that could be randomly assigned to your design problem. See what happens when you explore the possibilities of each attribute. The process also works well with verbs, such as "melt," "mend," "mock," or "magnify." From the sublime or the ridiculous to the profoundly practical, unfamiliar concepts are sure to emerge.

MAKE YOUR OWN FORCED CONNECTIONS

Apply intriguing attributes to designs for products, services, logos, typefaces, illustrations, or web themes.

Alien	Mechanical
Biomorphic	Nebulous
Colossal	Open
Disposable	Private
Edible	Queer
Fluffy	Religious
Grotesque	Skeumorphic
Heartbreaking	Therapeutic
Illegal	Utopian
Jumbled	Vulgar
Knotty	Wrong
Literate	Young
	Zoological

 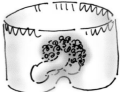

SKEUMORPHIC

A "skeumorphic" interface applies a metaphor from the physical world to a process in the digital world (such as using a trashcan to represent deleting files). These designs for skeumorphic underwear allow people to try on a different gender. Concept by Erica Holeman.

Illustrations by Jennifer Tobias

A great story does more than represent emotion from a distance. It makes us feel an emotional charge.

Act 2 | Emotion

CINDERELLA'S
EMOTIONAL
JOURNEY

Illustration by Ellen Lupton

ACT 2

Emotion

Why would you buy one pair of shoes instead of another? A runner will focus on comfort and ergonomics. A vegan will focus on materials. A bridesmaid will be searching for an awful shade of peach. Not all choices are so pragmatic, however. A pair of shoes could also trigger emotions, such as longing, lust, or painful memories of high school.

What shoes are you wearing now? Do you remember why you bought them? Maybe you liked their style, quality, or price, or their use of sustainable materials or fair labor practices. Since then, your emotional connection may have faded or deepened. Perhaps those shoes take you running or hiking, or they help you walk your dog or bike to work. Some day they will wear out, but maybe you'll buy a similar style later on, finding yourself attracted to a familiar stitch or texture. Products change the way we feel. Our relationships with them shift over time.

Designing for emotions requires thinking about how users will anticipate an experience and how they will remember it later. Will visitors to a hospital recall the warm fabrics and soft lighting of the waiting room or the harsh glare and sharp disinfectants? Will tourists who used a travel app remember how easy it was to find a train schedule, or will they recall a fake hotel review and a clumsy login process? Designers tap into people's emotions to trigger feelings of delight, desire, surprise, and trust.

Scientists and philosophers used to view emotions as sloppy, irrational impulses. Anger, love, and fear were considered inferior to critical analysis. Today, however, we talk about "emotional intelligence" as the ability to read people's feelings and respond in ways that build understanding and cooperation. Designers train their emotional intelligence by exploring empathy. They study the arc of a user's emotional journey in order to anticipate friction, offer rewards, and acknowledge errors in a friendly and compassionate way.

Designers can easily get trapped inside their own expert mindsets. To create products for an older person, a child, or someone with a disability or a different social background, designers need to build empathy with the user's values, aspirations, and culture. Design researcher Deana McDonagh explains, "Designers need to adopt strategies for accessing the emotional context of the products that they have to design for the people who will use them." In the process of co-design, design teams use a variety of research activities to establish empathy with users.

Emotions are adaptations that aid the survival of a species. Fear compels us to flee from danger, while love moves us to protect our young. Emotion triggers action. When we clench our fists, cringe in fear, dissolve into tears, or burst into song, we express emotion through physical gestures. Erupting spontaneously from the body, such gestures are common to blind people as well as sighted ones. These actions communicate feelings to the self and other creatures, making emotional life as profoundly social as it is individual.

The feelings provoked by a clunky shopping cart or a long wait at the dentist's office are likely to fall on the paler end of the emotional spectrum. When creating emotional journey maps, designers often indicate "good" and "bad" experiences with a happy or sad face. Designer Sherine Kazim thinks designers should look beyond this banal binary to address a more subtle range of emotions. For example, a game should generate surprise. An infographic about a natural disaster should acknowledge pain and grief. A meditation app should help users feel calm and centered. In Australia, the National Health Service successfully demanded that cigarette packages be designed to inspire fear and revulsion.

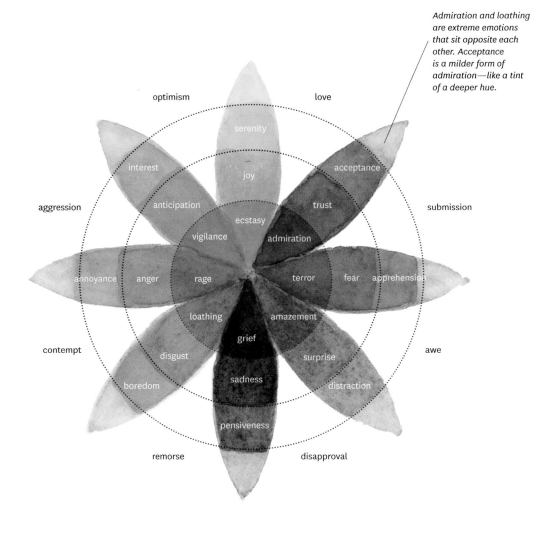

Admiration and loathing are extreme emotions that sit opposite each other. Acceptance is a milder form of admiration—like a tint of a deeper hue.

CHARTING EMOTIONS Psychologist Robert Plutchik designed a map of emotions inspired by color theory. He identified eight primary emotions, whose gradations and overlaps create dozens of variants. "Rage" and "terror" sit opposite each other, just as red and green face off on the color wheel. Each primary emotion varies in intensity, from "loathing" or "ecstasy" (extreme) to "boredom" or "serenity" (mild). Primary emotions mix to create secondary ones. "Awe" is a mix of "terror" and "amazement"; "love" is a cocktail of "joy" and "trust." Illustration by Jennifer Tobias. Adapted from Robert Plutchik, "The Nature of Emotions," *American Scientist* 89 (July–August 2001): 344–350.

BEGINNING
At the visceral level, design stirs an immediate reaction to form, color, texture, and materiality.

MIDDLE
At the behavioral level, design prompts a physical response or action.

END
At the reflective level, design engages memories and associations.

VISCERAL

BEHAVIORAL

REFLECTIVE

Now

Future

DON NORMAN'S
THREE LAYERS OF
USER EXPERIENCE

THREE LAYERS Don Norman's three layers of user experience overlap and mutually influence one another. Illustration by Jennifer Tobias. Adapted from Don Norman, *Emotional Design: Why We Love (or Hate) Everyday Things* (New York: Basic Books, 2004).

Emotions play a vital role in reasoning and ethical judgment. According to philosopher Martha C. Nussbaum, "Emotions are not just the fuel that powers the psychological mechanism of a reasoning creature, they are parts, highly complex and messy parts, of this creature's reasoning itself." Emotions are more than inner feelings. They are active, embodied responses to people, places, and events encountered in the world around us.

Emotions can be profound and transformative (grief when a loved one dies) or fleeting and mild (dismay when we drop a scoop of ice cream). Nussbaum calls strong emotions "geological upheavals of thought." They loom up in the moment like steep mountain peaks, confronting us with a sudden threat, loss, or opportunity. Milder emotions unfold gently in the background, like the general buzz of pleaure felt when talking with friends or walking in the woods. All creatures display emotions, from turtles and birds to cats and dogs. Even single-cell organisms exhibit primitive emotions— these microscopic creatures thrive and endure by evading predators and exploring their surroundings.

Emotions affect the design of anything from a font or a logo to a wireless speaker or a banking app. The success of a product lies not just in its basic utility but in its meaning in the lives of its users. When interaction design became a discipline in the 1980s and 90s, the field focused on how to keep people from getting frustrated by technology. The expression "don't make me think" became a battle cry for friction-free digital experiences. Today, emotion and pleasure as well as intuitive functionality are crucial elements of user experience.

Usability expert Donald Norman invites designers to generate wonder and surprise. He divided user experience into three phases: *visceral*, *behavioral*, and *reflective*. The visceral component is what we process right away with our minds and bodies. Here lie the sensuality of materials, the clash of colors, and the allure of form and texture. Behavior is an action users take—push a button, buy a book, read a caption, find the exit. Reflection is what we recall later, the emotional associations

MASLOW'S HIERARCHY [OF USER EXPERIENCE]

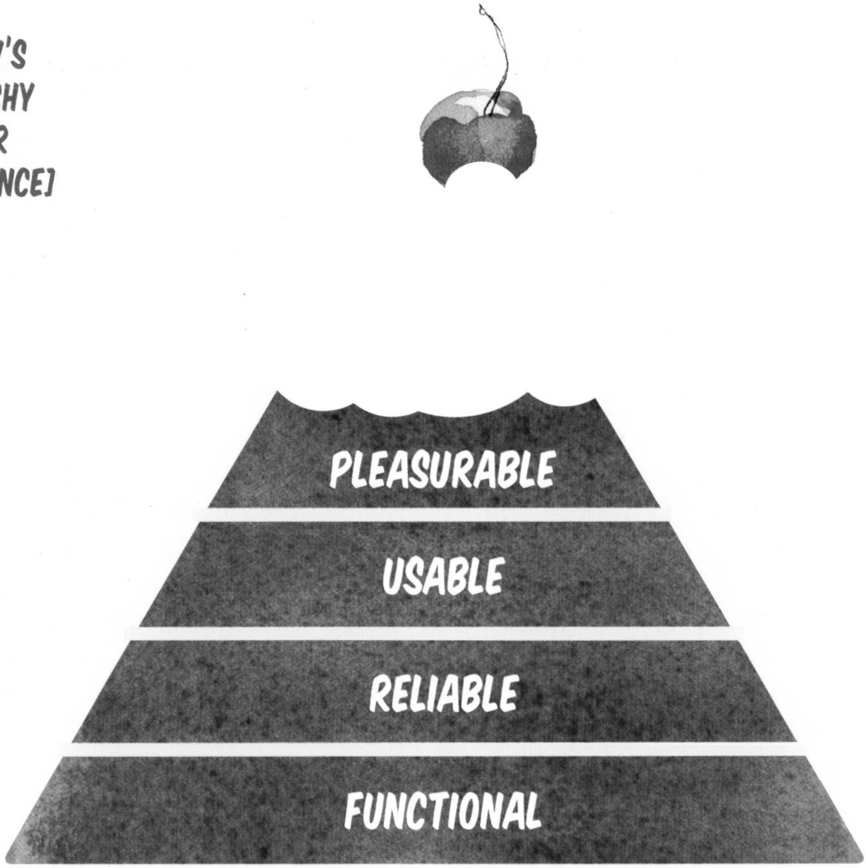

PLEASURABLE

USABLE

RELIABLE

FUNCTIONAL

HIERARCHY OF NEEDS The diagram above is based on Abraham Maslow's hierarchy of needs, a famous model of human psychology. According to Maslow, humans struggle to secure the essentials of survival (health, safety, and social acceptance). Only after securing these basic necessities can people attempt to grow and achieve happiness and self-actualization.

Designers Aaron Walter and Jared M. Spool applied Maslow's hierarchy to user experience. Their pyramid adds pleasure on top of such interaction design basics as function, reliability, and usability. Illustration by Jennifer Tobias. Adapted from Aaron Walter and Jared M. Spool, *Designing for Emotion* (New York: A Book Apart/Jeffrey Zeldman, 2011).

we forge with a product or service over time. "It is only at the reflective level," writes Norman, "that consciousness and the highest levels of feeling, emotions, and cognition reside." Norman's three phases of user experience recall the structure of storytelling: beginning/middle/end.

Emotions are often what move people to use a product. We turn to social media when we are hungry for love or validation. We peruse a news feed or watch cat videos to vanquish boredom or quell anxiety. Products can move users from one emotional state to another. An exciting story is a winding path of uncertainty and revelation. A story's emotional arc shifts over time. Designers use color, light, texture, and sound to modulate the mood of a product, service, or place. Allowing these elements to change in pace or intensity makes room for dips and rises in emotional energy.

Emotion is temporal. Waves of feeling drag us out of the present and into the past and future. Novelist F. Scott Fitzgerald wrote that trying to live in the present moment is a losing struggle. People, he said, are ceaselessly drawn to "the orgiastic future that year by year recedes before us." Mindfulness is a state of focused attention that requires people to resist distractions and stay focused on what is happening right now. Mindfulness is difficult to sustain because the mind is a creature of history, constantly wandering back and forth in time. Achieving mindfulness may yield deep psychic rewards, but memory and anticipation are essential to the human condition. Past and future are integral elements of full, temporally complex experiences.

READ MORE Martha C. Nussbaum, *Upheavals of Thought: The Intelligence of Emotions* (New York: Cambridge University Press, 2001); Deana McDonagh and Cherie Lebbon, "The Emotional Domain in Product Design," *The Design Journal* 3 (2000): p31–43; Sherine Kazim, "An Introduction to Emotive UI," Huge Inc, http://www.hugeinc.com/ideas/perspective/an-introduction-to-emotive-ui, August 18, 2016; accessed December 29, 2016.

Experience Economy

In the twenty-first century, designing and selling experiences eclipsed the manufacture of physical things. An experience stirs emotions and generates memories.
It embraces dramatic action, sensory engagement, and temporal interaction with users. During an experience, users create meanings and associations that become more important than the event itself.
The **experience economy** has changed the way commercial companies design and deliver products. The experience economy has also changed how schools, hospitals, museums, and other organizations provide services to communities.

	COMMODITY	PRODUCT	SERVICE	EXPERIENCE
ECONOMY	Agrarian	Industrial	Service	Experience
ECONOMIC FUNCTION	Extract	Make	Deliver	Stage
NATURE OF OFFERING	Fungible (interchangeable)	Tangible	Intangible	Memorable
KEY ATTRIBUTE	Natural	Standardized	Customized	Personal
METHOD OF SUPPLY	Stored in bulk	Inventoried after production	Delivered on demand	Revealed over time
SELLER	Trader	Manufacturer	Provider	Stager
BUYER	Market	User	Client	Guest
FACTORS OF DEMAND	Characteristics	Features	Benefits	Sensations

THE RISE OF THE EXPERIENCE ECONOMY Table adapted from B. Joseph Pine II and James H. Gilmore, *The Experience Economy* (Cambridge: Harvard Business Review Press, 2011).

Experience Economy

EXPERIENCE BOOM In the late 1990s, the term *experience economy* became the banner of a business revolution. Customers and employees became players in scripted dramas. Narrative eclipsed physical things.

The word "experience" appears over 125 times in this book. This term ricocheted through the business world with the publication of *The Experience Economy* in 1998. According to authors B. Joseph Pine II and James H. Gilmore, a new economic order was gripping affluent societies. The "experience economy" had overthrown the service economy of the 1950s and 60s, created when businesses like banks and insurance companies became more important than manufacturing.

Pine and Gilmore were fascinated by the rise of Starbucks. Why, they asked, were people willing to pay so much for a cup of coffee, which could be bought for next to nothing at the corner deli? Here's why: Starbucks wasn't just selling coffee; it was selling an *experience*. Deli coffee is cheap, convenient, and indistinguishable from the same cup sold down the street for the same price. An experience isn't just consumed in the moment. It engages consumers in a theatrical performance, creating a lasting memory and an emotional bond.

The Starbucks drama begins when a customer passes through the portal of the cafe and plunges into a curated world of sounds, smells, graphics, lighting effects, and furnishings. An elaborate lingo of beverage sizes and hot and cold concoctions indoctrinates users in a secret language, while servers and customers act out a sacred ritual. By writing names on customers' cups, the cashier initiates personal contact, while the barista puts on a show replete with explosive auditory effects. The environment hums with social activity and the sounds and smells of making, stimulating desire and inviting a longer stay.

Theatricality drives experiences like this one. For the authors of *The Experience Economy*, theater is not just a metaphor. Theater is real. When actors perform, they connect with an audience. The cashier, the barista, and the customer take part in a living drama. They play their roles in real time, following a script to convey action and intention.

When a person buys a service, he purchases a set of intangible activities carried out on his behalf. But when he buys an experience, he pays to spend time enjoying a series of memorable events that a company stages—as in a theatrical play—to engage him in an inherently personal way.

B. JOSEPH PINE II AND JAMES H. GILMORE, *THE EXPERIENCE ECONOMY*

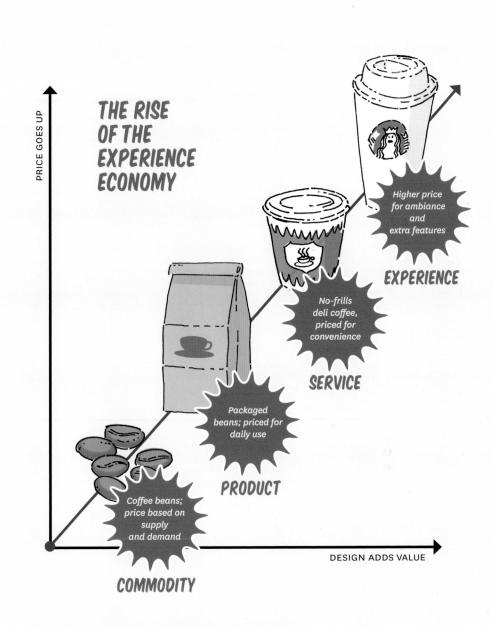

THE RISE
OF THE
EXPERIENCE
ECONOMY

PRICE GOES UP

Higher price for ambiance and extra features

EXPERIENCE

No-frills deli coffee, priced for convenience

SERVICE

Packaged beans; priced for daily use

PRODUCT

Coffee beans; price based on supply and demand

COMMODITY

DESIGN ADDS VALUE

FROM COMMODITY TO EXPERIENCE As a product progresses from a mere commodity to a full-bodied experience, it employs more design features—and becomes more expensive. An experience is a memorable event staged like a theatrical play. Graph and chart adapted from Pine and Gilmore, *The Experience Economy*. Illustration by Jennifer Tobias.

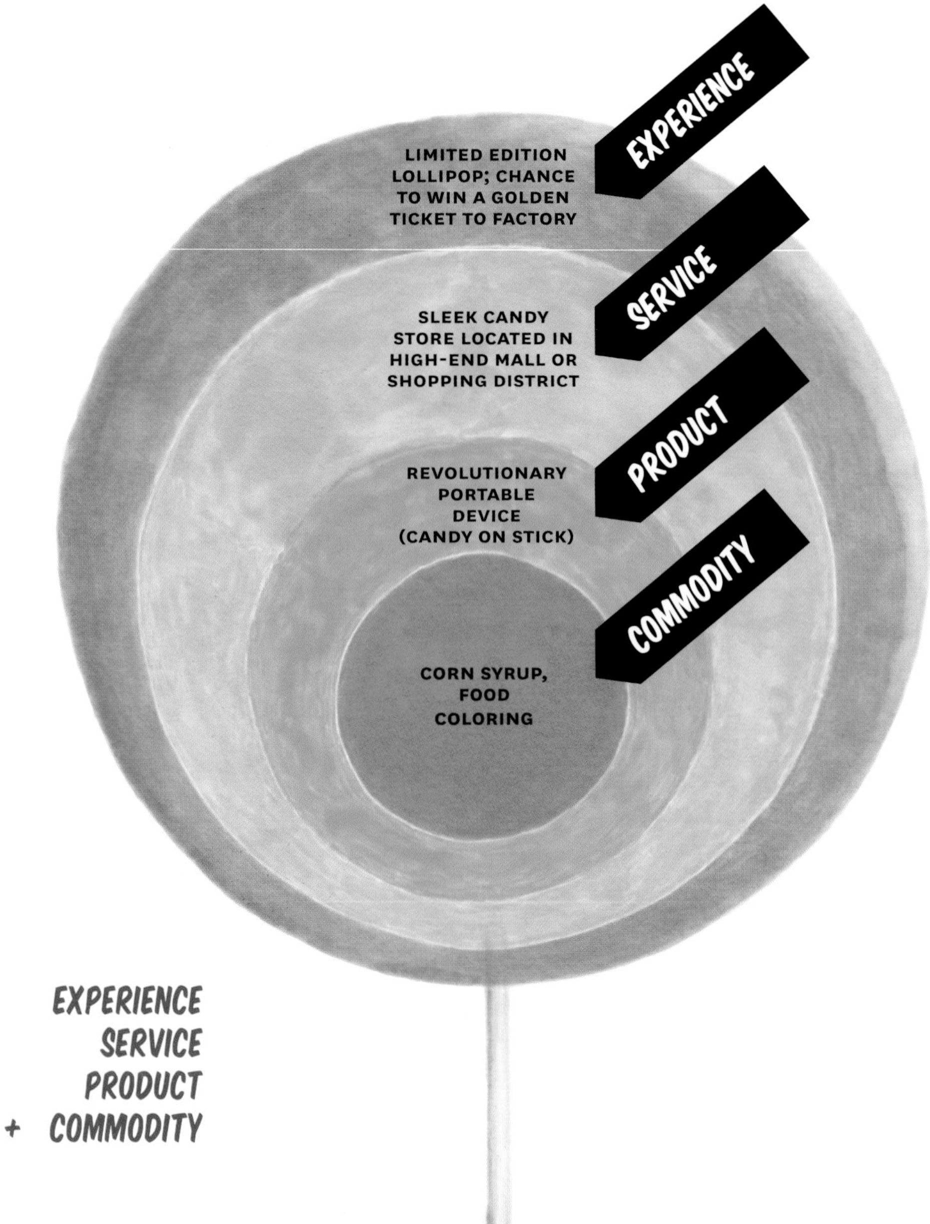

EXPERIENCE

**LIMITED EDITION
LOLLIPOP; CHANCE
TO WIN A GOLDEN
TICKET TO FACTORY**

SERVICE

**SLEEK CANDY
STORE LOCATED IN
HIGH-END MALL OR
SHOPPING DISTRICT**

PRODUCT

**REVOLUTIONARY
PORTABLE
DEVICE
(CANDY ON STICK)**

COMMODITY

**CORN SYRUP,
FOOD
COLORING**

*EXPERIENCE
SERVICE
PRODUCT
+ COMMODITY*

RIPPLE EFFECT Many contemporary products combine aspects of services, experiences, goods, and commodities. A smartphone is a commodity (using raw materials), wrapped inside a product (phone and basic OS), wrapped inside a service (carrier's plan), wrapped inside an experience (ecosystem of apps and add-ons). Illustration by Jennifer Tobias.

READ MORE Albert Boswijk, Thomas Thijssen, Ed Peelen, and S. B. Thomas, *The Experience Economy: A New Perspective* (Amsterdam: Pearson Prentice Hall, 2007); Brenda Laurel, *Computers as Theater* (New York: Addison Wesley, 1993); Alessandra Stanley, "A Wine of One's Own? They'll Drink to That," *New York Times*, July 2, 2016, http://nyti.ms/29aquZy; cited July 2, 2016.

Experience Economy

SHIFTING PARADIGMS What has changed since *The Experience Economy* appeared in 1998? In today's social and digital landscape, users play more active roles. Contemporary brands are more participatory and less top-down.

Experiences are created when designers shift emphasis from objects to actions. Pine and Gilmore call this process *ing the thing*. Imagine a car ad showing a driver gliding along coastal roads and narrow European streets, or a promotion for a restaurant chain showing people laughing with friends over steaming boats of pasta, or a college brochure depicting young people from diverse backgrounds chatting thoughtfully under big trees. Cars become driving. Food becomes dining. Education becomes learning.

Like a story, an experience takes place over time. It has a beginning, middle, and end, and it activates emotions and senses. *The Experience Economy* applies Freytag's narrative arc to a trip to the mall or a day at Disneyland. Pines and Gilmore adopted this narrative diagram from Brenda Laurel's book *Computers as Theater*, which uses the dramatic arc to explain human/computer interactions. *The Experience Economy* makes scant reference to "design," yet this influential book derives one of its core principles from design theory. The terms "experience design" and "user experience" (UX) have since entered the mainstream of design discourse.

Pine and Gilmore separated services from experiences. In practice, however, services and experiences tend to blur together. Once upon a time, phone systems delivered little or no emotional value to their customers. Now, a smartphone is a product, a utility, and a commercial platform for digital products. Choosing a carrier and a service plan has become a subtle process orchestrated via sophisticated websites, branded retail centers, lavish advertising, and carefully scripted sales pitches.

Another big shift is the transformation of experiences into two-way exchanges between people and products. Designers use techniques of co-creation to involve users in shaping products and places. Customers use social media to build the meaning of brands and to conduct their own conversations around value and identity. Consumers have more power to punish brands that have objectionable business practices, political views, or environmental policies.

Today, nearly every service is also an experience. Service design has become a specialized field that fits business processes to the needs and wants of users.

No luxury firm can ignore the accelerating shift from "having" to "being."

BOSTON CONSULTING GROUP, QUOTED BY ALESSANDRA STANLEY

TOOL

Emotional Journey

While a plot is the series of events that make up a story, an **emotional journey** consists of the feelings those events inspire. Stories have highs and lows. They shift in energy and tempo, sometimes moving fast, sometimes moving slow. A person's relationship with a product or service changes over time. Energy rises and falls as users feel curiousity, pleasure, and satisfaction. Users may also hit negative patches of doubt, frustration, and anger.

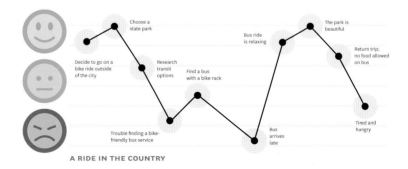

A RIDE IN THE COUNTRY

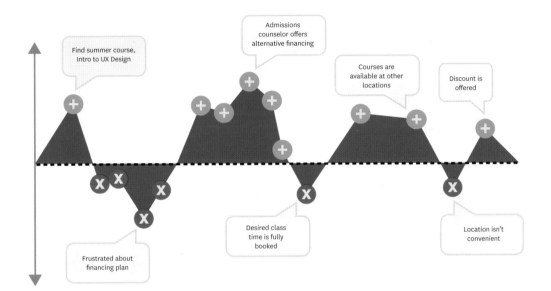

A RIDE IN THE COUNTRY (left) Adapted from Tom Voirol, "Rethinking Customer Engagement Touch Points to Deliver Enhanced Guest Experience and Drive," April 10, 2014, http://www.slideshare.net/readingroom/digital-hotel-guest-experience-tom-voirol-at-fha2014-food-hotels-asia-conference; accessed June 4, 2016, CC Attribution.

TEMPLATE (above) Ready-made templates make it easy to create journey maps to share with clients and stakeholders. This one is adapted from a PowerPoint template designed by SlideModel, https://slidemodel.com/templates/customer-journey-map-diagram-powerpoint/; accessed June 6, 2016.

Emotional Journey

MISERY AND ECSTASY In 1947, a young writer named Kurt Vonnegut was studying anthropology at the University of Chicago. In his graduate thesis, he argued that all stories can be mapped as a line moving up and down between misery and ecstasy.

The University of Chicago rejected Vonnegut's thesis, but he went on to write some of the most acclaimed books of his generation, including *Slaughterhouse Five* (1969) and *Breakfast of Champions* (1973). These satirical novels combine realism, science fiction, and deadpan wit.

Years later, Vonnegut delivered humorous lectures about the diagrams he had made as an earnest young man in graduate school. Drawing on a chalkboard, he graphed generic plots, like "Man in the Hole" and "Boy Meets Girl." Many stories start with positive emotions and then dip down into danger and despair. A man falls in a hole (bad fortune), and the people of the town save him (good fortune). A boy meets a wonderful girl (happiness), but then he loses her (misery). When the boy and girl get back together, the graph shoots up to the top of the chart.

Designers create emotional journey maps analogous to Vonnegut's graphs. Curt Arledge argues that an experience designer is also a "memory designer." People return to a product or place because they have positive memories about

it. In order to help people produce those positive memories, the designer plans an experience whose emotional arc reaches points of intensity, similar to the peaks in a good story. The arc needs to end in a satisfying way. An appropriate ending for an online article might be a well-curated list of related articles; a poor ending would be a grid packed with phony click bait or a pop-up window begging for the reader's email address.

To create an emotional journey map, designers observe users and break down their experience into steps. Some steps in the journey are positive, while others are negative. Designer Garron Engstrom explains that emotional journey maps help designers "lean in to the user's emotions," anticipating lows as well as highs. Graphing users' emotions is a tool for understanding and improving a person's relationship with a product or service. Designers can create their own formats for visualizing the customer journey, or they can download a variety of templates with preset options and prompts.

BAD TO WORSE In 2016, a team of data scientists in Vermont put Vonnegut's theory to a statistical test. They studied over 1,700 stories and found that their emotional arcs conformed to six basic shapes. Yet Vonnegut's funniest graphs are those that fail to follow an expected pattern. In Kafka's *Metamorphosis*, a miserable, unpopular young man who hates his job and dislikes his family wakes up one day to discover, alas, that he is a cockroach. His story starts low and keeps sinking lower. The graph never ever ticks up.

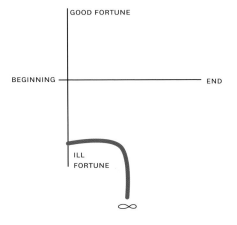

KURT VONNEGUT'S EMOTIONAL JOURNEY

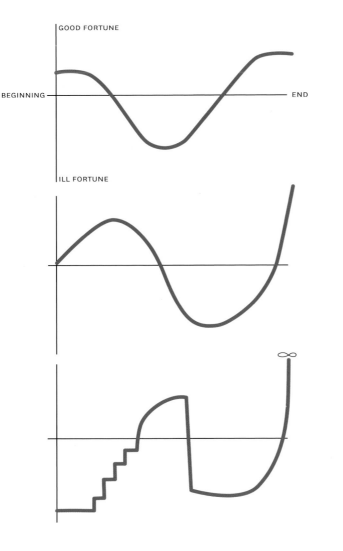

GOOD FORTUNE

BEGINNING

END

ILL FORTUNE

MAN IN THE HOLE
*Man falls in the hole.
The people of the
village rescue him.*

BOY MEETS GIRL
*Boy meets girl, loses
her, and gets her back.*

CINDERELLA
*Sad, orphaned girl
can't go to the ball. She
gets help from Fairy
Godmother, attends the
ball, loses her slipper, and
marries the prince.*

READ MORE Kurt Vonnegut, *A Man Without a Country* (Random House, 2005); Geoffrey Johnson, "Kurt Vonnegut in Chicago: Some Footnotes," ChicagoMag. com (March 19, 2012), http://www.chicagomag. com/Chicago-Magazine/The-312/March-2012/ Kurt-Vonnegut-in-Chicago-Some-Footnotes/; accessed June 4, 2016; Curt Arledge, "User Memory Design: How to Design for Experiences That Last," *Smashing Magazine*, August 1, 2016, https://www. smashingmagazine.com/2016/08/user-memory-design-how-to-design-for-experiences-that-last/?ref=mybridge.co; accessed September 2, 2016; Garron Engstrom, "Principles of Emotional Design," http://www.slideshare.net/garrone1/principles-of-emotional-design (July 25, 2015); accessed June 4, 2016; Neil Gains, "User Journey Maps," DoctorDisruption.com (July 18, 2014), http://www. doctordisruption.com/design/design-methods-21-user-journey-maps/; accessed June 4, 2016.

Emotional Journey

PAIN POINTS Where are the highs and lows in the story of Cinderella? How does the story end? Imagine that Cinderella's fairy godmother is a digital product. What ratings would this fictional app earn for customer experience?

Emotional journey maps are useful for finding pain points and communicating results. "The map should honestly reflect the reality of interactions with a business," says usability expert Neil Gains, "including the good and the bad, and moments of indecision, confusion, frustration, delight, neutrality, and closure." Journey maps often follow the experience of a typical persona, identifying touchpoints between user and product, from first learning about it to getting it and trying it.

Let's turn Vonnegut's graph of the Cinderella story into a map of customer satisfaction. Cinderella starts out miserable: she has nothing to wear and she can't go to the ball, so she downloads the Fairy Godmother app. Fairy Godmother gets five stars for the shoes, the dress, and the tiara. Fairy Godmother's transportation arrangements get high marks, too—she turns a herd of mice and a big pumpkin into an elegant horse and carriage. The customer journey takes a nosedive, however, when the clock starts striking twelve. Cinderella rushes down the stairs to the parking lot, losing a glass slipper along the way. The magical carriage turns back into an ordinary pumpkin.

A service designer or product designer will be hard-pressed to restore Fairy Godmother's five-star rating after Cinderella returns to her life of drudgery. Perhaps Fairy Godmother can compensate with a new perk or special feature, such as a lost-and-found service that uses GPS tracking to return missing possessions to their rightful owners. (After Cinderella gets her slipper back, she opens her own 3D-printed custom shoe shop and lives happily ever after in financial independence.)

Stories without conflict are dull. Although users don't expect to experience terror or rage during a trip to a furniture store or a ride home from a party, their journey shouldn't be flat. Waiting two hours for a flight to Denver is a low-energy experience; boarding the flight with a huge backpack and a cranky boyfriend requires high energy. Restaurants and airports fill wait times with breadsticks and newsstands so people never get bored. Arledge says that brief slowdowns in a digital processs can indicate that the system is working ("optimizing your file," "reviewing your request"), thus conveying quality. Designers can create value from moments of rest, reflection, and anticipation.

Creating emotional high points might just mean the difference between a product that's perceived as smooth but forgettable and one that's flawed but awesome and leaves people with a lasting positive impression.

CURT ARLEDGE, "USER MEMORY DESIGN"

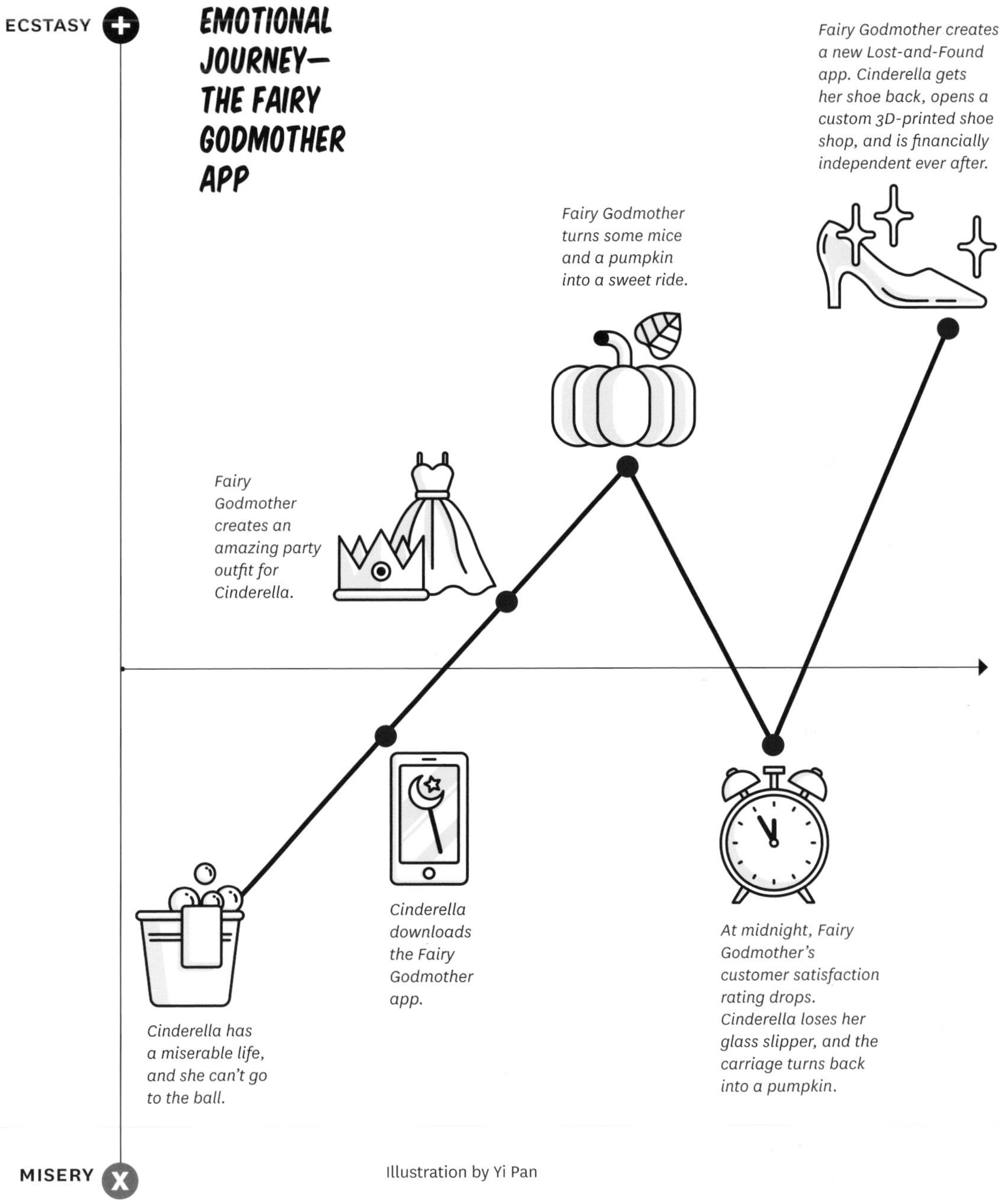

ECSTASY **+**

EMOTIONAL JOURNEY— THE FAIRY GODMOTHER APP

Fairy Godmother creates a new Lost-and-Found app. Cinderella gets her shoe back, opens a custom 3D-printed shoe shop, and is financially independent ever after.

Fairy Godmother turns some mice and a pumpkin into a sweet ride.

Fairy Godmother creates an amazing party outfit for Cinderella.

Cinderella downloads the Fairy Godmother app.

Cinderella has a miserable life, and she can't go to the ball.

At midnight, Fairy Godmother's customer satisfaction rating drops. Cinderella loses her glass slipper, and the carriage turns back into a pumpkin.

MISERY **X**

Illustration by Yi Pan

Emotional Journey

HOT AND COLD Where are the points of greatest intensity in an experience? How does an experience end? Highs and lows contribute to how people remember—and evaluate—a product, service, or performance.

How an experience comes to a finish affects how people judge the overall event. Psychologist Daniel Kahneman calls this phenomenon the *peak-end rule*. The most intense part of an experience (the peak) as well as the conclusion (the end) influences whether people would choose to repeat that experience in the future. This phenomenon has been observed in various situations, from waiting in line for theater tickets to taking a vacation or getting a colonoscopy. Waiting in line makes people irritable and annoyed; if the line starts moving quickly toward the end of the process, however, people will view the whole experience more favorably.

In a study of pain, subjects placed one hand in cold water for sixty seconds. Then they did the same thing again, but this time for thirty seconds longer. During that extra half-minute, however, the water gradually warmed up, giving the experience a happier ending. Asked to repeat one of the two sessions, subjects chose the longer one, which seemed less uncomfortable to them because it had ended well.

Experience designers pay special attention to how an action concludes, offering a bit of emotional bling to reward users for their time and effort, such as applying a discount code at checkout and seeing their bill magically decrease.

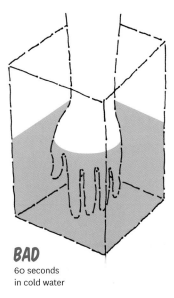

BAD
60 seconds
in cold water

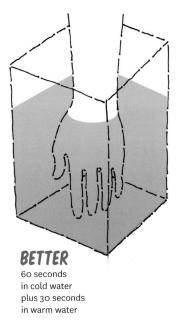

BETTER
60 seconds
in cold water
plus 30 seconds
in warm water

Illustration by Jennifer Tobias

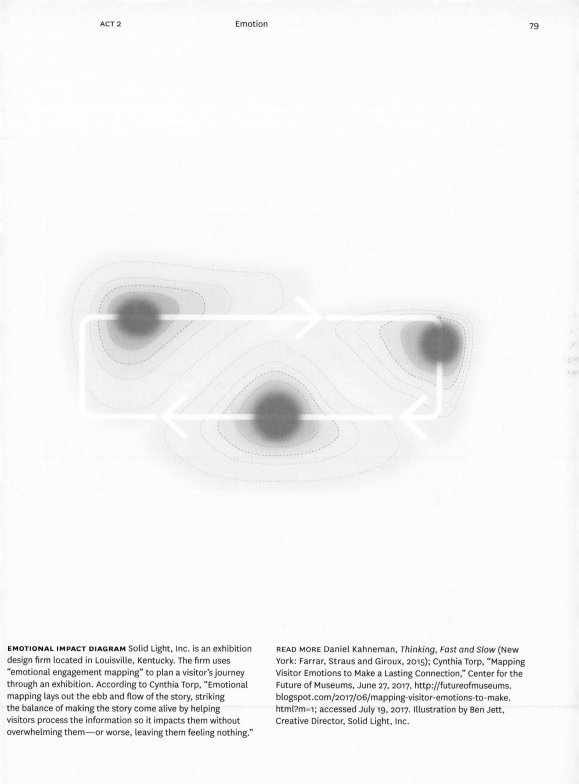

EMOTIONAL IMPACT DIAGRAM Solid Light, Inc. is an exhibition design firm located in Louisville, Kentucky. The firm uses "emotional engagement mapping" to plan a visitor's journey through an exhibition. According to Cynthia Torp, "Emotional mapping lays out the ebb and flow of the story, striking the balance of making the story come alive by helping visitors process the information so it impacts them without overwhelming them—or worse, leaving them feeling nothing."

READ MORE Daniel Kahneman, *Thinking, Fast and Slow* (New York: Farrar, Straus and Giroux, 2015); Cynthia Torp, "Mapping Visitor Emotions to Make a Lasting Connection," Center for the Future of Museums, June 27, 2017, http://futureofmuseums. blogspot.com/2017/06/mapping-visitor-emotions-to-make. html?m=1; accessed July 19, 2017. Illustration by Ben Jett, Creative Director, Solid Light, Inc.

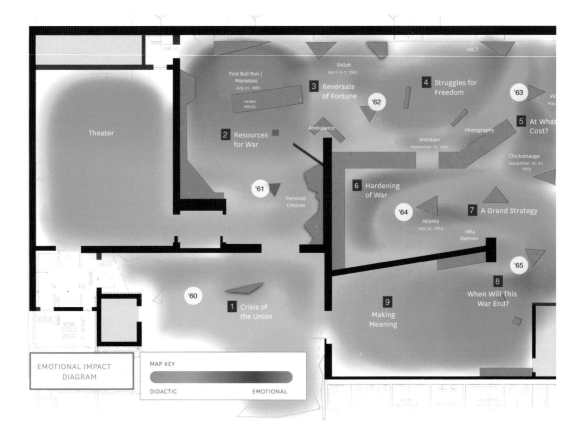

USCT

First Bull Run /
Manassas
July 21, 1861

HENRY
HOUSE

Shiloh
April 6–7, 1862

3 Reversals
of Fortune

'62

4 Struggles for
Freedom

'63

Vic
May

Theater

2 Resources
for War

Ambulance

Photography

5 At What
Cost?

Antietam
September 17, 1862

Chickamauga
September 18–20
1863

'61

6 Hardening
of War

Personal
Choices

'64

Atlanta
July 22, 1864

7 A Grand Strategy

1864
Election

'65

8

'60

1 Crisis of
the Union

9
Making
Meaning

When Will This
War End?

EMOTIONAL IMPACT
DIAGRAM

MAP KEY

DIDACTIC   EMOTIONAL

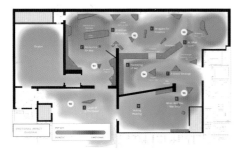

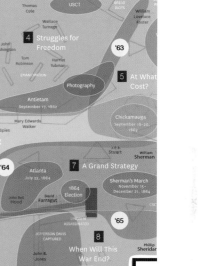

THEMATIC BUBBLE
DIAGRAM

EMOTIONAL IMPACT DIAGRAM A team of designers, curators, and historians set out to create a major exhibition about the U.S. Civil War for the American Civil War Museum in Richmond, Virginia. The team sought to present a more personal view of an historic event that is usually represented in military and political terms. Ben Jett, creative director at Solid Light, Inc., had tried various ways to graph emotional journeys. Here, he decided to map the intensity of the exhibition layout with a heat map.

Jett also created a bubble diagram that indicates the exhibition's main themes. The heat map and bubble map allowed the team to plan where the exhibition's peak areas of conflict and drama would occur—and where visitors would be able to step back and pause. The tools also helped the team plan their use of resources and invest more project funds in the areas of greatest impact. Illustrations by Ben Jett, Creative Director, Solid Light, Inc.

TOOL

Co-creation

When developing a new product, service, or app, designers often seek knowledge from users. Co-creation activities range from evaluating existing solutions to generating new ideas. In co-creation, designers work with users in order to understand the context of a project and learn how new solutions could improve people's lives. When users play an active role in the design process, they become expert witnesses to a human task or challenge. A range of exercises—from focus groups to brainstorming sessions—help prompt discussion, stimulate creative thinking, and build empathy between designers and users.

Illustration by Jennifer Tobias

Co-creation

EMPATHY The ability to recognize and share the mental states of others is called *empathy*. Designers often create content and services for people unlike themselves. Designers develop empathy through role playing, interviews, and observation.

A novel or film builds empathy by transporting readers into someone else's frame of mind, letting an audience see life through the eyes of an heiress, an orphan, or a refugee. Empathy enables people to work together and construct societies for mutual benefit. Empathy is essential for human civilization, and it is the linchpin of user-centered design.

Deborah Adler runs a design firm in New York City that specializes in healthcare products. She shadows nurses to understand their points of view. "Nurses," she says, "are my teachers." In one project, Adler was commissioned by a maker of medical supplies to redesign their packaging for a urinary catheter. Her new package aimed to reduce the high rate of hospital infections associated with this common procedure. Adler began by talking with nurses and observing them at work. She learned that the old packaging was awkward and illogical—the tools were crammed in wherever they fit, rather than reflecting the order in which nurses use them and the space required for using them properly. (The packaging includes a tray that provides a sterile work area for this bedside procedure.)

Adler recalls, "The new package that we designed worked well, but the nurses were tossing away the patient education part of the kit." So she added an illustrated, Hallmark-type card with the patient information inside, printed on luxurious, uncoated stock. The card is placed where it can't be missed, and is now less likely to be overlooked. It is special and personal, and nurses don't throw it away. Patients put the card on the bedside table, where it also serves to educate the family. "By touch alone, the card was perceived as a thing of value for the patient," Adler says. "We transformed patient education from something forbidding into something welcome."

PATIENT EDUCATION When Deborah Adler redesigned Medline's Foley Catheter packaging, she presented instructional informaton for patients on a card printed in full color on beautiful paper. The card was valued by patients, families, and nurses, supporting crucial patient learning. Illustration by Jennifer Tobias.

DEANA MCDONAGH'S GUIDE TO EMPATHIC DESIGN

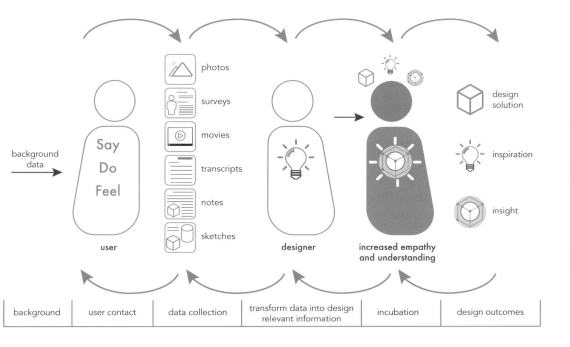

DESIGNING EMPATHY Deana McDonagh's diagram of the design process includes users at the earliest phases of research. She has explored numerous ways that designers can build empathy with users, including photographic and video documentation, surveys and questionnaires, and sketches observed in the field. Illustration by Deana McDonagh.

Co-creation

RECALL, ANALYZE, AND INVENT Co-creation encompasses numerous modes of participation. Users might describe their own situations, analyze a problem, or propose new solutions. Dissecting prior experiences and current beliefs primes users to imagine the future.

A participatory design session often begins with uncovering people's desires and opinions about a life activity, such as taking the bus, visiting a museum, or feeding a cat. A group conversation is preceded by one or more quick warm-up activities; these are often completed individually, not in teams. "Homework" done prior to the session can also be helpful, such as filling in a diary or survey, or photographing a living or work space.

After warming up and briefly discussing the results, the group can now tackle a larger activity. Some activities are analytical, such as listing the pros and cons of a given solution or telling stories about real or imagined scenarios.

Marketing teams often ask focus groups to respond to a given product or concept. Typical activities include comparing or ranking proposed solutions, or evaluating the cultural associations or emotional appeal of a new design. In order to seek more creative input from users, designers work as peers and equals within communities. The user becomes an expert in the subject being studied. Building this relationship requires tools that stimulate creativity and inspire users to generate new knowledge.

CO-CREATION | Warm-up Exercises

SURVEY OR QUESTIONNAIRE Each participant answers questions on a worksheet at the beginning of the event. Types of question include multiple choice, rankings, and short answers. The survey can also be used to collect demographic information.

DIARY OR JOURNAL Ask participants to record the elements of a routine activity, such as "feeding cat" or "commuting to work." The diary could also span an entire day, such as tracking participants' interactions with their pets from dawn to bedtime, or tracking all modes of transit used in a single day. If completed as "homework," photos can be used as well as text.

MOOD BOARD Designers often collect a patchwork of references to set the tone of a project. Called *mood boards*, such collections can also help focus groups communicate visually about a subject. The process can be freeform, using magazines or old books as random source material, or more structured, using images preselected by the design team.

WORD MAP To begin the exercise, each participant writes a topic at the center of a page. In a process of quick free association, participants draw or write associated concepts to create clusters of ideas. Diagram by Erica Holeman.

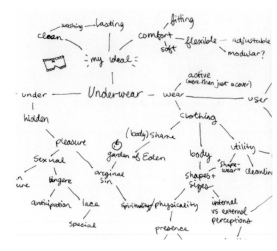

READ MORE Elizabeth B.-N. Sanders and Pieter Jan Stappers, *Convivial Toolbox: Generative Research for the Front End of Design* (Amsterdam: BIS Publishers, 2012); Joe Langford and Deana McDonagh (2003) "Focus Group Tools," in *Focus Groups: Supporting Effective Product Development*, Langford and McDonagh (London: Taylor and Francis, 2003), 173–224.

CO-CREATION | Creative Thinking Exercises

POSITIVES AND NEGATIVES This exercise looks at forces that are hindering and helping a desired change, such as "getting more people to take the bus to work." The moderator draws a chart with two columns: helping and hindering, or pros and cons. The group generates lists of positive forces ("save money," "save planet") and negative forces ("buying tickets is hard," "bus is often late"). The activity helps the team recognize and address the pain points in a process.

FIRST-PERSON NARRATIVE Participants imagine an ideal product or system by describing how they would use it in real life. ("The bus stops in front of my favorite coffee shop. Once an hour, a bus arrives that is reserved for cyclists. There is room on the bus for everyone's bike.")

ASSOCIATION Here, participants assign emotions or personalities to a product or idea. This can be done by free-associating or by matching the product with a set of cards printed with words or pictures.

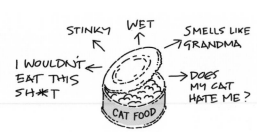

Illustrations by Jennifer Tobias

Co-creation

INVENTING A BETTER CAT FEEDER Talking to users about an automatic cat feeder revealed insights about humans, cats, and smelly food. Users shared their opinions, exposed their emotions, and discovered potential problems with the proposed design.

Eric Lima and Alan Wolf are proud cat lovers. They are also professors at The Cooper Union School of Engineering in New York City. They had an idea for a new automatic cat feeder. They saw that most existing products on the market are designed for dispensing *dry* food, but none was successfully serving *wet* food. (Wet food is a healthier choice for cats but makes a bigger mess for humans.) Wolf and Lima have invented an app-controlled cat feeder that will open a sealed package of food (ensuring that the food is served fresh) and then move the discarded portion to an enclosed area for disposal later (ensuring that the uneaten food doesn't sit out all day). The inventors created a working prototype of the device in their engineering lab, but to make the product real they sought to collaborate with professional designers.

Lima and Wolf brought their prototype to Stuart Harvey Lee, founder of the industrial design firm Prime Studio, who insisted that the next step in the design process was to get feedback from users. First, the team engaged a market research firm to conduct an online survey, posing general questions to four hundred cat owners. Next, the design team held a series of in-person focus groups, where they showed participants drawings of potential designs for the new cat feeder.

Some participants were skeptical about using an automatic feeder until they heard others talking about its potential merits—no more sticky, stinky food bowls to handle, no more wake-up yowls in the middle of the night, no more worries about working late or going away for the weekend. Participants also pondered the emotional needs of their feline companions. Would the feeder be scary? Could it greet the cat with voice messages from its special humans? Would cats attack the unit and tamper with the food packets stored inside? Overall, participants thought the machine would function better for both cats and people if it were used every day, not just on special occasions.

The design team—hearing that cat owners expected to use the device on a daily basis—knew that the machine would have to be small enough to leave out all the time without taking over the kitchen. The focus groups revealed that cat owners, especially those with higher incomes, were interested in the automatic feeder once they knew that it would be clean, safe, compact, and convenient. (Thus the product's success will depend on customer education.)

If designed well, the new cat feeder could be more than a gadget. It could make feedings easier for humans while creating a healthy and consistent routine for kitties. The app could educate owners about how much to feed their cats. And wait, there's more! Equipped with a webcam, the product could send confirmation photos when meals are successfully delivered and devoured. And maybe it could snap cat selfies, too—adding an extra helping of emotional delight to a practical pet-care product.

I sleep less now that I have a cat. FOCUS GROUP PARTICIPANT

DIARY OF A FOCUS GROUP

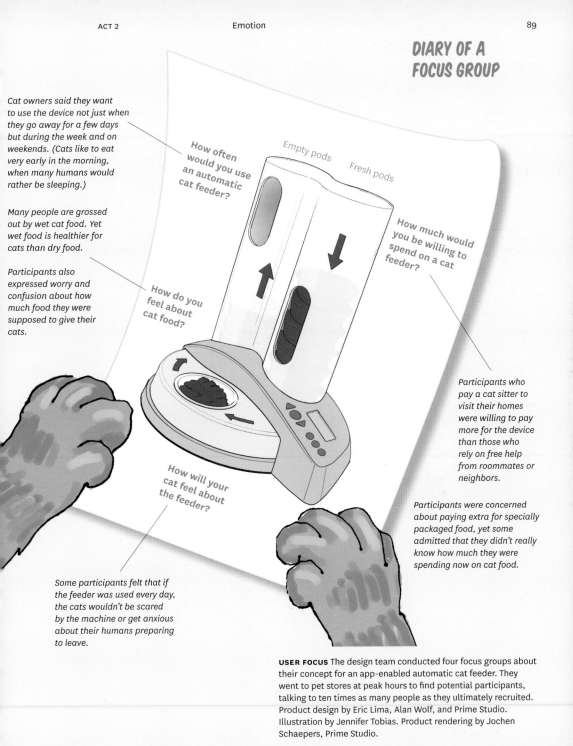

Cat owners said they want to use the device not just when they go away for a few days but during the week and on weekends. (Cats like to eat very early in the morning, when many humans would rather be sleeping.)

Many people are grossed out by wet cat food. Yet wet food is healthier for cats than dry food.

Participants also expressed worry and confusion about how much food they were supposed to give their cats.

How often would you use an automatic cat feeder?

Empty pods   Fresh pods

How much would you be willing to spend on a cat feeder?

How do you feel about cat food?

Participants who pay a cat sitter to visit their homes were willing to pay more for the device than those who rely on free help from roommates or neighbors.

Participants were concerned about paying extra for specially packaged food, yet some admitted that they didn't really know how much they were spending now on cat food.

How will your cat feel about the feeder?

Some participants felt that if the feeder was used every day, the cats wouldn't be scared by the machine or get anxious about their humans preparing to leave.

USER FOCUS The design team conducted four focus groups about their concept for an app-enabled automatic cat feeder. They went to pet stores at peak hours to find potential participants, talking to ten times as many people as they ultimately recruited. Product design by Eric Lima, Alan Wolf, and Prime Studio. Illustration by Jennifer Tobias. Product rendering by Jochen Schaepers, Prime Studio.

TOOL

Persona

An archetypal user of a product or service is
called a **persona**. Like a character in a novel or
film, each persona is trying to get something
done. Design teams use personas to imagine
how different people with different desires
and abilities will experience your tool or
service. The characteristics of a persona can
include general demographics (such as gender,
age, and income) as well as specific quirks and
interests (such as collecting antique cars or
growing heirloom melons). The most valuable
personas are based on observing real people.
Personas play starring roles in *scenarios*, short
stories built around achieving a specific goal.

PEOPLE, PLACES, THINGS When Emily Joynton set out to create
a narrative comic about living with her intense roommates in
Miami, she began by creating portraits of each character. Her
portraits use words and images to build up an understanding
of the person. Illustration by Emily Joynton.

THE DISCO BALL SOMEHOW FELT SYNONYMOUS WITH NICO. HE USED IT IN A PERFORMANCE PIECE, OWNED AT LEAST ONE, AND HAD A PERS-ONALITY TO MATCH THE SUBTLY SPARKLY OBJECT. WHEN WE HAD PARTIES DOWN IN OUR BASEMENT, A COUPLE TINY DISCO BALLS WOULD ALWAYS TURN UP THE NEXT MORNING.

FOR ABOUT HALF THE YEAR WE LIVED TOGETHER, NICO SLEPT ON A PULL-OUT COUCH (BUT NOT ON THE PULL-OUT PART, ON THE ACTUAL CUSHIONS). HE COMPLAINED OF BACK PAIN AND EVENTUALLY GOT THIS FOAM WEDGE TO HELP HIS BACK. I THOUGHT HE WAS BEING A BIG BABY ABOUT THE WHOLE THING BUT NOW HAVING HAD BACK PAIN MYSELF, I FEEL BAD FOR NOT TAKING HIM SERIOUSLY.

WHEN OUR LEASE WAS UP AND NICO DECIDED TO MOVE OUT, THERE WAS A LOT OF MISCOM-MUNICATION AND RESE-NTMENT INVOLVED IN THE PROCESS. LONG STORY SHORT: A COUPLE OF MY NEW ROO-MMATES AND I GOT SO FRUSTR-ATED WITH THE WHOLE THING THAT IN RETALIATION WE STOLE THE WHEEL OFF OF NICO'S TRUCK TO GIVE HIM A TASTE OF THE SAME INCONVENIENCE WE WERE FEELING IN THIS ENTIRE MOVE-OUT ORDEAL. IN HINDSIGHT, I'M SURE THERE WAS A BETTER WAY EV-ERYONE COULD HAVE HANDLED THE TRANSITION.

Persona

PEOPLE WITH GOALS The process of creating personas and scenarios helps a design team work with their users in mind and build empathy. What do people actually want? What will enhance their lives? What challenges do they face?

One persona is not enough. Design teams create several personas in order to think about a range of users. These personas become archetypes representing different needs, abilities, and levels of interest. Naming the personas makes them more real and memorable. Critiquing design solutions from the perspectives of different personas helps designers think beyond their personal likes and dislikes or their own creative investment in a given concept and begin to see it from a user's point of view ("What would Rob do?").

At the start of a project, designers, ethnographers, or researchers talk with users and observe them in different settings. They compile their observations and then look for patterns within the data. How do shared issues or interests form into clusters? When will users need extra help achieving their goals?

The "nuclear family" depicted in vintage TV commercials is rare in modern life and never reflected broad social realities. Designers at IDEO recommend considering "extreme users" as well as so-called "average" ones. A person who is deeply obsessed with a subject—such as video games, gardening, or grilling whole pigs—will enjoy talking about their passion and will have surprising ideas. Important insights will also come from a person who has an impairment, such as low vision or limited hand strength. If a product or service can be valuable to extreme users, then it will likely work for those with more middle-ground interests and abilities.

The design team creates a document that tells a story about each persona, giving them names, backgrounds, and visual portraits. Like characters in a movie or short story, personas are active. They have behaviors and values, desires and hangups. They shouldn't be sterotypical. Designer Christof Zurn created the Persona Core Poster, a template for creating user profiles. Turn the page to see our template, a simpler worksheet created for beginners, inspired by Zurn's work.

The use of personas in the design process was invented by Alan Cooper, a pioneer in the field of interaction design and cofounder of Cooper in San Franscisco. Alan Cooper's first persona was a project manager named Kathy, a fictional character based on a real worker he had interviewed while developing a complex piece of office software in 1983. As he was producing the software, Cooper found himself having imaginary conversations with Kathy inside his head. By asking her about her needs and actions in different situations, he was able to make the software more useful. Cooper continued to create personas and described the method in his influential book, *The Inmates Are*

READ MORE Schlomo Goltz, "A Closer Look at Personas and How They Work," *Smashing Magazine (*August 6, 2014), https://www.smashingmagazine.com/2014/08/a-closer-look-at-personas-part-1/; accessed July 8, 2017; Alicia Clegg, "Harnessing the Power of Extreme Customers," *Financial Times* (January 6, 2014), https://www.ft.com/content/f7256696-746e-11e3-9125-00144feabdc0?mhq5j=e2; accessed July 8, 2017; Alan Cooper, "The Origin of Personas," Cooper.com (May 5, 2008),

https://www.cooper.com/journal/2017/4/the_origin_of_personas; accessed July 9, 2017; Alan Cooper, *The Inmates Are Running the Asylum: Why High Tech Products Drive Us Crazy and How to Restore Sanity* (London: Sams-Pearson Education, 2004); "Scenarios," Information & Design, http://infodesign.com.au/usabilityresources/scenarios/; accessed July 9, 2017.

Running the Asylum. Cooper says, "Personas, like all powerful tools, can be grasped in an instant but can take months or years to master." With practice, they become powerful devices for thinking about design problems; they also help designers talk about their process with team members and clients.

Once the design team has created personas, it's time to write *scenarios*—short narrative sketches in which characters seek to fulfill a goal, such as registering for a cooking class or finding a bus schedule. Scenarios are concise and schematic. Rather than going into detail about every button a user pushes or how many menus and dialogue boxes they open, the scenario focuses on the main purpose of each action. For example, "Beth searches online for a Chinese cooking class. She can't find a course that meets on the weekends, but she finds one that meets on Tuesday nights; she enrolls." Different personas will have different scenarios: "Bill, who uses a wheelchair, wants to take cooking lessons near public transit. The app doesn't say whether the classes are accessible, so he has to call each provider until he finds one."

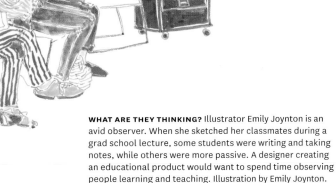

WHAT ARE THEY THINKING? Illustrator Emily Joynton is an avid observer. When she sketched her classmates during a grad school lecture, some students were writing and taking notes, while others were more passive. A designer creating an educational product would want to spend time observing people learning and teaching. Illustration by Emily Joynton.

Persona

STUDY HABITS We created personas for three archetypal users of FlashKard, a hypothetical learning app for middle school students. Each learner has different abilities, obstacles, and goals. Their scenarios describe the context for achieving their goals.

PERSONA + SCENARIO WORKSHEET

NAME

Pick a name that is easy to remember.

DESCRIPTION

Name a trait, such as The Hoarder, The Explorer, or The Maker.

BACKSTORY

List characteristics and experiences such as education, nationality, work history, hobbies, and family life.

RESOURCES

Is the persona an expert or a novice? What abilities or resources do they have, and what obstacles do they face?

EMOTIONS

How does the persona feel about the challenge? Anxious or confident, excited or bored?

GOALS

What action does the persona want to complete?

SCENARIO

Write and/or sketch a scenario about how the persona accomplishes their goal.

PERSONA WORKSHEET Inspired by "The Persona Core Poster," Creative Companion (May 5, 2011), https:// creativecompanion.wordpress.com/2011/05/05/the-persona-core-poster/. Creative Commons Attribution Share-Alike.

ROB | THE BUILDER

BACKSTORY Rob lives in a small apartment with his grandmother, a registered nurse.

RESOURCES Rob enjoys STEM subjects and wants to design bridges when he grows up. Rob has a mobile phone but no computer at home. He would rather draw maps and diagrams and build models than listen to lectures.

EMOTIONS Rob is very confident and sometimes impatient. He makes careless mistakes and forgets to check his work.

GOAL Rob wants to study for a statewide math competition.

SCENARIO Rob always finishes early during class. During his extra time, he makes FlashKards of the problems he just completed. Creating the cards is fun, and it gives him a chance to check his work and find mistakes.

LISA | THE CHAMP

BACKSTORY Lisa is a competitive runner. She lives with two parents, two siblings, and two dogs in a two-story townhouse.

RESOURCES Lisa plans to be a varsity athlete in high school. She dreams of a college sports scholarship. Lisa often travels long hours on the bus with her team and has to be at school early to train. In class, she is often sleepy or physically restless.

EMOTIONS Lisa is anxious about her prechemistry course. She believes she is "bad at science" and will never succeed at STEM subjects.

GOAL Lisa wants to find more time to study while keeping up with her training.

SCENARIO Lisa creates FlashKards after she finishes each homework problem. On the morning of the test, she turns on the app's audio screen-reading feature and listens to her FlashKards during her morning run and on the team bus.

SOO-JIN | THE FARMER

BACKSTORY Soo-Jin recently moved to the U.S. from Korea with her parents. Their apartment complex has a community garden.

RESOURCES Soo-Jin likes growing vegetables and being outdoors. She plans to become a climate scientist. Soo-Jin has impaired hearing and wears hearing aids. She excels at math and science once she has mastered a concept, but she finds lectures challenging.

EMOTIONS She feels overwhelmed when the classroom is loud. She sometimes struggles with English and feels isolated.

GOAL Soo-Jin wants to study outdoors with other people.

SCENARIO Soo-Jin and a classmate make FlashKards together and play games to learn them. Soo-Jin uses the app's translation feature to reinforce the meaning of new words.

Illustrations by Irina Mir

Persona

Character Studies From beauty products to tech gadgets, every product has a personality. Materials, colors, shapes, and graphics engage the senses, influence our behavior, and tell stories about social identity.

Characters are the driving force of stories. If a product or brand was a character, what would it say and how would it move? Would its voice be girlish or vampy, silly or maternal? Would it run, jump, dance, saunter, or lie on its back and wag its tail? People instinctively assign personality traits to inanimate things. Shape, color, texture, and materials contribute to a product's personality. So does brand language, from the product's name to the mountains of copy that explain and promote it. Behavior matters, too. A gold smartphone or a fancy sports car begs to be pampered and protected; a paperback book or a family minivan invites casual use. Designers can explore and refine a product's personality throughout their process.

Can a plastic water bottle achieve status as a sustainable product? The designers of Fred, a line of bottled water, sought to create a form factor so appealing, people would save and reuse the bottle instead of throwing it away. Fred is shaped like a "hip flask," a reusable container designed for stashing whiskey or bourbon in a man's pants or jacket pocket. Thus Fred's handy, functional shape invokes the subversive pleasures of an intimate masculine subculture. The product's name—set in four letters of solid, American gothic type—amplifies the manly vernacular of the brand. Fred is relaxed, manly, and (maybe) sustainable.

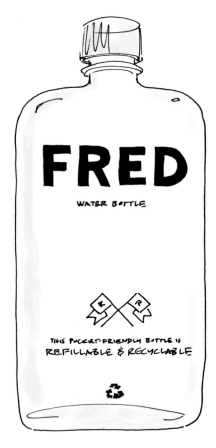

READ MORE Ruth Mugge, Pascale C. M. Govers, and Jan P. L. Schoormans, "The development and testing of a product personality scale," *Design Studies* 30 (2009): 287–302.

Illustration by Jennifer Tobias.

PRODUCT PERSONALITY PROFILE— TWO WIRELESS SPEAKERS

A warm, dimmable LED light inside the glass cylinder resembles a candle flame; this product is expensive.

Zipper allows users to change the bright cover; this product is moderately priced.

	PROFILE #1	PROFILE #2
	Libratone ZIPP Mini wireless speaker	SONY Glass wireless speaker

TARGET USER		PROFILE #1	PROFILE #2
	AGE	25	45
	OCCUPATION	programmer	fashion buyer
	HOUSING	urban apartment	3-bedroom townhouse
	TRANSIT	bicycle	BMW
	PERSONALITY	dynamic/extrovert	organized
	VACATION	hiking	Euro-camping
	HOME STYLE	IKEA and thrift	upscale contemporary
	CLOTHING	jeans and vintage	Club Monaco

PERSONALITY TEST How can you understand a product's personality? Try asking users what they think. Give participants a questionnaire featuring images of various items, such as a car, a coffee maker, or an audio device. The questionnaire asks them to imagine the intended user of each product and conjure a lifestyle surrounding it. How old is this person? Where would they spend their vacations? What job would they have? Where would they live? Was the product designed for a person similar to them, or for someone quite different? Finally, would the personality profile encourage the particpant to choose or reject the product? Use the questionnaire as the basis of a longer discussion. Diagram adapted from A. Bruesberg and Deana McDonagh-Philp, "New product development by eliciting user experience and emotions," *International Journal of Human Computer Studies* 55 (2001): 435–52. Illustration by Jennifer Tobias.

WHAT GENDER IS IT?

Illustrations by Jennifer Tobias

His, Hers, or Theirs? Some products are designed for everyone, with no special features evoking masculine or feminine personality stereotypes or social norms. When designers assign gender qualities to a product, they might make it more appealing to some users—but risk excluding others.

Lip balm used to be a product designed for everyone. A slim, black tube of Chapstick is a neutral, utilitarian commodity. Yet women are more likely than men to purchase lip balm. The founders of EOS (Evolution of Smooth) decided to appeal directly to female users by delivering lip balm in a new format. EOS has a sculptural shape that feels good in the hands and is easy to find inside a big handbag.

While EOS addresses the desires of a specific audience, some people object to the idea of creating products for specific genders. Such products can alienate people who identify as nonbinary. Others feel that gendered products are wasteful and reinforce stereotypes. MUJI is one of several brands that create beautiful self-care products that are gender neutral.

The color pink wasn't always associated with the female sex. In the United States, pink became popular for women during the presidency of Dwight D. Eisenhower. His wife, Mamie Eisenhower, caused a fashion sensation when she wore a pink gown to the 1952 inaugural ball. A few pink products have evaded gender tyranny, including strawberry ice cream, fiberglass insulation, and Pepto-Bismol, the creamy cure-all for indigestion.

Names for everything from house paint to eye shadow can contain the seeds of a story. Designer Franki Abraham points out that names for nail polish colors often say more about character and action than about the colors inside the bottles. Nail polish is worn and enjoyed by persons of any gender, but the cosmetics industry tends to presume a female subject.

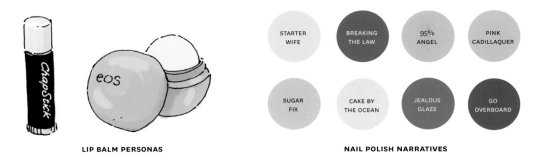

LIP BALM PERSONAS

NAIL POLISH NARRATIVES

LIP CARE FOR LADIES In focus groups, women reported that their tiny tubes of Chapstick often went missing in the cavernous depths of their purses. Women were interested in applying lip balm from a pot rather than a stick, but using their fingers seemed unhygienic. EOS founder Sanjiv Mehra says, "The products that women depend on every day should deliver moments of delight that elevate these daily routines." Pretty colors, exotic flavors, and themed collections make the product fun to use and keep customers interested.

READ MORE Elizabeth Segran, "The Untold Story of How Lip Balm Upstart EOS Outdid Chapstick," *Fast Company*, October 19, 2016; https://www.fastcompany.com/3063333/startup-report/the-untold-story-of-how-lip-balm-upstart-eos-outdid-chapstick; accessed December 29, 2016; Jennifer Wright, "How did pink become a girly color?" *Vox* (14 April 2015), https://www.vox.com/2015/4/14/8405889/pink-color-gender; accessed August 1, 2017.

TOOL

Emoji

Every moment of every day, millions of people around the world are communicating with emoji. These digital images of people, things, and tasty snacks originated in Japan, where teenagers in the 1990s went wild exchanging bit-mapped symbols on their pagers and flip phones. Today, many operating systems and native apps for iOS and Android have custom emoji fonts. A panel of Unicode officials decides whether new emoji can be admitted to the pantheon. Proposals are rejected if—among other criteria—they are too specific ("spicy tuna" rather than "sushi" in general), too trendy ("Brooklyn beard"), or too branded ("Adidas," "Nike," or "Jimmy Choo"). Creating expressive icon systems fuels a broader area of design practice.

HAND-PAINTED EMOJI Type designer Colin Ford is fascinated by the history of emoji and their unique design potential. Straddling the space between type and image, these tiny characters enrich conversation in a society of constant texting. Ford has begun creating his own family of hand-painted emoji. Shown here are the first nine. He has approximately 2,657 more characters to go.

READ MORE Colin Ford, "Emoji: A Lovely History" (May 13, 2016), https://medium.com/making-faces-and-other-emoji/emoji-a-lovely-history-1062de3645dd; accessed July 25, 2017; "Submitting Emoji Proposals," http://unicode.org/emoji/selection.html; accessed July 25, 2017.

TRASH BOT (above) Wael Morcos and Jon Key designed this character for the exhibition *See, Hear, Play: Designing with Sound*, organized by Cooper Hewitt, Smithsonian Design Musem. Morcos and Key created a kit of parts to illustrate the different emotional states of this imaginary street-cleaning machine. The character and icon set were designed to accompany an interactive sound-design activity. The designers used simple geometric shapes to express different emotional states. As Trash Bot consumes more bottles and cans, the creature's body gets taller. Design by Wael Morcos and Jon Key, Morcos Key.

ARTHUR (right) Eddie Opara designed Arthur as a character that communicates information about energy consumption and the environment on kiosks installed throughout an elementary school. When students ask Arthur simple questions, Arthur displays the answers on his screen. His color and facial expression change depending on how much energy the school is consuming and how much students have been interacting with him. The color palette maps intuitively to Arthur's moods. His simple face consists of two dots and a surprisingly expressive line. Design by Eddie Opara, Pentagram.

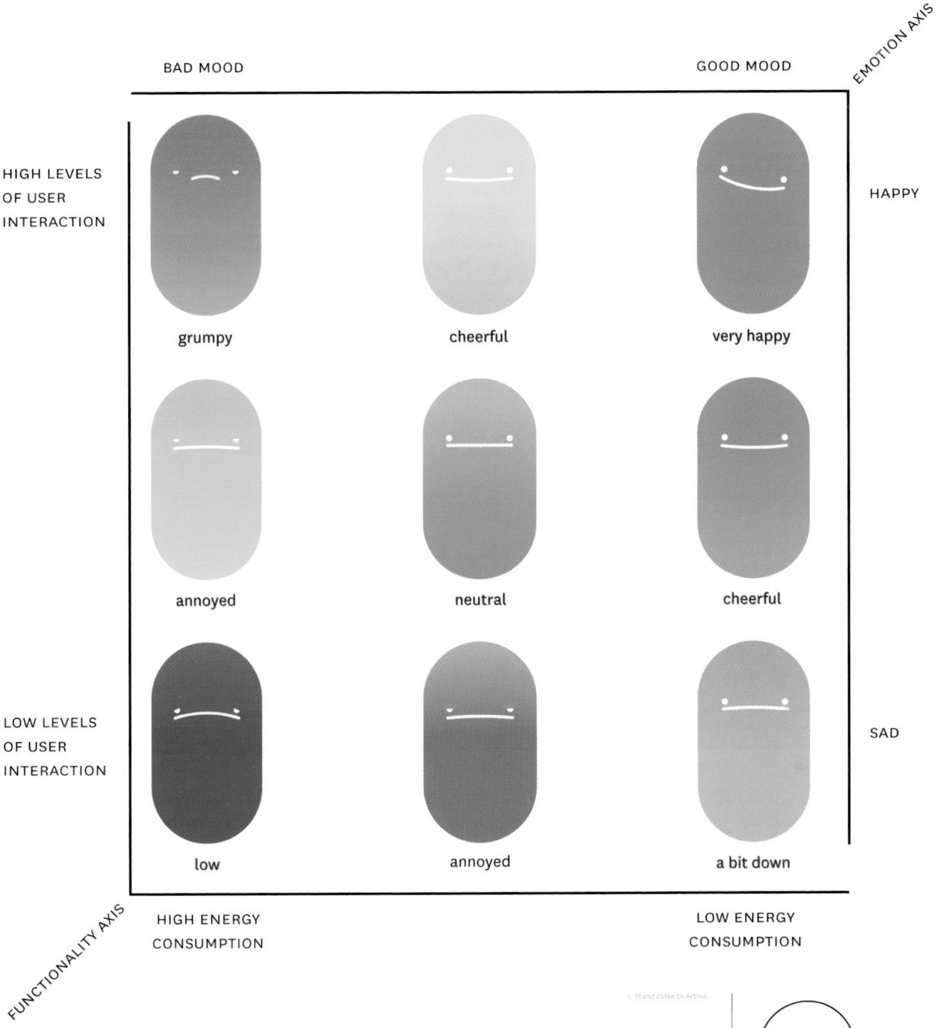

EMOTION AXIS

	BAD MOOD		GOOD MOOD	

HIGH LEVELS
OF USER
INTERACTION

HAPPY

grumpy   cheerful   very happy

annoyed   neutral   cheerful

LOW LEVELS
OF USER
INTERACTION

SAD

low   annoyed   a bit down

FUNCTIONALITY AXIS

HIGH ENERGY   LOW ENERGY
CONSUMPTION   CONSUMPTION

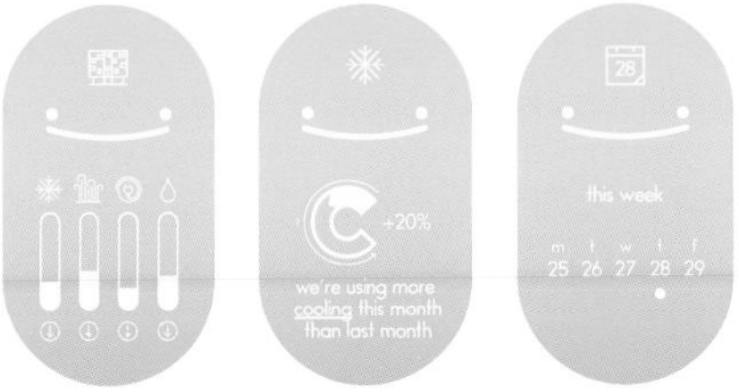

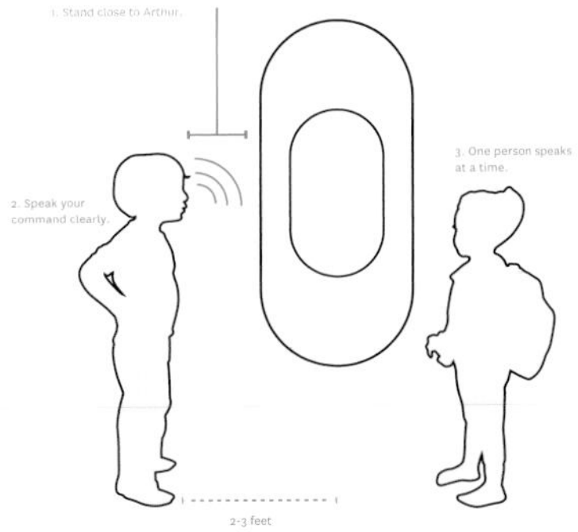

1. Stand close to Arthur.

2. Speak your command clearly.

3. One person speaks at a time.

2-3 feet

we're using more cooling this month than last month

+20%

this week
m t w t f
25 26 27 28 29

TOOL

Color and Emotion

Red can represent love and sexuality or
violence and bloodshed. It can also mean
stop, *do not enter*, or *rejected password*. In
addition to conveying such culturally specific
meanings, color can trigger responses that
seem hardwired in the human psyche.
Combining **color and emotion** is a powerful
storytelling tool. Color creates a sensory
impression that reflects mood and emotion.
A color climate that is clean and bright
feels different from one that is airy and
pale or muted and dark. Designers explore
color's cultural context, narrative content,
and psychological effects in order to alter
the meaning of an image, environment, or
product—and change its impact on users.

WESTERN FAIRY TALES:
LOVE, SEXUAL MATURITY

GREEK MYTHOLOGY:
MARS, GOD OF WAR

CHINA AND JAPAN:
LOVE, LUCK, HAPPINESS

SHINTO RELIGION (JAPAN):
LIFE

REVOLUTIONARY RUSSIA:
SOCIALIST STATE

UNITED STATES:
REPUBLICAN PARTY

CHINA, INDIA, AND NEPAL:
BRIDAL WEAR

GLOBAL ISO STANDARDS:
STOP, DO NOT ENTER

NATIONAL FLAGS: BLOOD
SHED FOR INDEPENDENCE

WORLDWIDE: BLOOD OF
THE COCHINEAL BEETLE

WORLDWIDE: FIRE

GERMANY, POLAND, RUSSIA:
FEAR, JEALOUSY

KOREA: LOVE, ADVENTURE,
GOOD TASTE

WORLDWIDE:
COCA COLA

READ MORE Victoria Finlay, *Color: A Natural History of the Palette* (New York: Random House, 2002); Zena O'Connor, *Colour Symbolism: Individual, Cultural, and Universal* (Sydney Australia: Design Research Associates, 2015); Ruben Pater, *The Politics of Design* (Amsterdam: BIS Publishers, 2016).

CLEAN WELL
BOTANICAL DISINFECTANT

GREENSHIELD
LAUNDRY DETERGENT

EMG
MULTIPURPOSE CLEANER

FROSCH BIO SPIRIT
WINDOW CLEANER

ECO-ME NATURAL
CLEANING SPRAY

ECOVER
MULTIPURPOSE SPRAY

GREAT VALUE NATURAL
LAUNDRY DETERGENT

SUN CHIPS FRENCH ONION
WHOLE GRAIN CHIPS

PURITY GREEN
AUTO WASH

DR EARTH
EXOTIC BLEND PREMIUM SOIL

SEVENTH GENERATION
FREE AND CLEAR TAMPONS

PURITY PRODUCTS
NUTRITIONAL SUPPLEMENTS

GREEN CUISINE
PACKAGED RICE DINNER

TLC
MULTIPURPOSE SPRAY

METHOD KIDS
SQUEAKY GREEN BODY SOAP

SIMPLE GREEN
ALL-PURPOSE CLEANER

Color and Emotion

WHAT DOES GREEN MEAN? The color green means life and plenitude pretty much anywhere on Earth where plants grow. In product marketing, the color green is a symbol of ecosensitivity and care for the environment.

Greenwashing is the practice of using language, color, and other branding elements to convince consumers that a product is healthy for people or good for the environment. Shades of green have become so strongly linked to earth-friendly, nontoxic products, some consumers buy goods in green packages without reading the fine print. The color alone has an emotional impact, providing a gentle "nudge" to buy. Filling a green plastic bottle with detergent or window cleaner makes consumers feel more healthy and virtuous; it does little, however, to control waste.

Although greenwashing is a dubious practice, the positive emotional effects sparked by greenness could be reason enough—in some situations—to employ this ubiquitous symbol of nature and life.

Ruzica Stamenovic studied the impact of green branding in several Singapore hospitals that had earned environmental architecture certifications. Meeting such rigorous standards helps the planet, but it doesn't do much for patients or visitors if they don't know about it. An energy-saving heating system is not a tangible part of a patient's experience. Yet knowing that a hospital is committed to the environment and to the natural landscape can enhance well-being. Stamenovic found that placing a park bench inside a hallway or painting a mural of falling leaves in a windowless waiting room helped people feel connected to nature. Offering representations of nature throughout an entire facility—not just in dedicated pockets of outdoor space—made people feel more attuned to nature and aware of the institution's green values.

Could looking at a picture of a verdant landscape help a person heal? The health of patients in a psychiatric ward improved when photos of landscapes were hung on the walls in place of abstract art or nothing at all. (Take that, Kandinsky.) Watching videos of nature not only helped patients deal with pain and remain optimistic about their conditions but helped them lower their blood pressure and heart rates.

Artificial nature could help out in dreary workplaces as well. In an experiment conducted at the University of Melbourne, subjects sat at computers completing a dull but brain-intensive task. After working for five minutes, they took a short break while an image popped on the screen. The image was either a photograph of a concrete rooftop or a photograph of a rooftop covered with green plantings. After returning to work, subjects in the concrete rooftop group began making more errors and showed signs of diminished focus, while the subjects who had taken a "green microbreak" continued to perform well and even improve. According to environmental psychologist Kate Lee, people are spontaneously drawn to images of nature and thus focus on them with little effort. Thus such images help conserve the mental resources required for concentration. Taking your dog outside could help, too!

READ MORE Dhruv Khullar, M.D., "Bad Hospital Design Is Making Us Sicker," *New York Times* (February 22, 2017); Ruzica Bozovic Stamenovic, "Branding Environmental and Evidence Based Hospital Design," 30th International Seminar for Public Health Group (PHG) of the Union of International Architects (UIA) at Kuala Lumpur Convention Centre, 2010; Nicole Torres, "Gazing at Nature Makes You More Productive: An Interview with Kate Lee," *Harvard Business Review* (September 2015): 32–33.

TOOL

Color and Emotion

HOW DO PEOPLE REACT TO COLOR? Although color has different symbolic meanings in different cultures, scientific research suggests that in the absence of other cues, some responses are nearly universal, or widely shared among many people.

Why do orange, yellow, and red make us feel alive and alert, while blue calms us down? This reaction may be deeply rooted in the species' quest for survival. Long before creatures could see the colors of the rainbow, says color vision scientist Jay Neitz, ancient organisms developed receptors that register the yellowness or blueness of light. Each of these colors of light has a different wavelength. Human beings still have these receptors—called *melanopsin*—which help us know the time of day. Sensing night and day is a crucial skill for countless living things, from single-celled organisms to sophisticated predators.

Our deep-seated reaction to blue and yellow may underscore broader emotional responses. We instinctively see yellow as the color of happiness because it is the color of sunshine and waking life. Blue is connected with peacefulness and rest, a mode of being that is also necessary for survival. According to Neitz, "The reason we feel happy when we see red, orange, and yellow light is because we're stimulating this ancient blue–yellow visual system." Although a relentless parade of emoji and smiley faces has reinforced yellow's happiness quotient, that doesn't mean the relationship is wholly arbitrary. The equation of yellow and happiness bears the weight of biological truth.

A study of color, emotion, and music, conducted with subjects in Mexico and the United States, sought to find out if different qualities of music trigger relatively consistent emotional responses in people, and if those same responses correlate closely with qualities of color. Participants identified a quick, upbeat piece by Bach as happy and energetic, while tagging a lower, slower composition by Brahms as moody and sad. They associated Bach with light, bright, warm colors, while linking Brahms to duller, deeper, cooler tones.

Such research confirms the instincts of many artists and designers. Most of us know that bright, warm colors suggest happiness and joy, while cool hues and dull, shadowy tones are more downbeat. A mix of perceptual and cultural factors makes the fit of colors and emotions feel right.

A psychologist and a designer asked another question: how might color stimulate users of a product or interface to feel or act a certain way? Their research suggests that reds, yellows, and oranges tend to prompt an activated, energized state of mind in users, while cooler blues and purples are linked to calmness or focus.

Studies like these suggest that not only can color *represent* an emotion or mood, but color could—under optimum circumstances—lead people toward *experiencing* that mood. A compelling story inspires people to feel emotions, not just to witness them. Narrative helps us shuttle between representation and experience, between cultural convention and embodied, felt response.

READ MORE Yasmin Anwar, "Back to the Blues, Our Emotions Match Music to Colors," *Berkeley News* (May 16, 2013), http://news.berkeley.edu/2013/05/16/musiccolors/; accessed June 6, 2017; Alan Manning and Nicole Amare, "Emotion-Spectrum Response to Form and Color: Implications for Usability," Conference proceeding, IEEE (July 19–22, 2009); Stephen Palmer et al. "Music–Color Associations Are Mediated by Emotion," *Proceedings of the National Academy of Sciences of the United States of America* 110.22 (2013): 8836–8841; Natalie Wolchover, "Your Color Red Really Could Be My Blue," *Live Science* (June 29, 2012), https://www.livescience.com/21275-color-red-blue-scientists.html; accessed July 30, 2017.

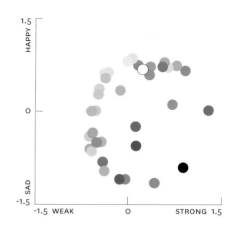

EMOTIONAL PALETTE In a study linking music, emotion, and color, researchers created a remarkably subtle color palette to share with participants. Rather than pick hues straight from a basic box of crayons, they assembled an array of swatches that vary in lightness and saturation. Participants were asked to evaluate the emotional tenor of the colors independently as well as relating the colors to short passages of music. Partcipants tended to link happy music and upbeat emotions with lighter, brighter, warmer colors, while linking sadder music and lower emotions with duller, darker, cooler tones.

This multidimensional scale shows the participants' response to correlating a selection of colors with eight emotional terms. The colors vary in intensity as well as in hue. The emotions selected for the study also vary in intensity (happy, sad, angry, calm, strong, weak, lively, and dreary). The study evaluated the emtional tone and intensity of music as well as color. Music has a more direct and immediate emotional impact than color. Graph redrawn from Palmer et al.

COLORWAYS Textile designers often apply different colors to a single pattern design, allowing them to create multiple products from one set of printing plates. Such color ranges are called *colorways.* Changing the color of a pattern can change its mood. To create the designs shown here, Alexander Girard provided the manufacturer with watercolors of the pattern and hand-painted swatches. Patterns are often uses as backgrounds or textures

that recede on a wall, garment, package, or digital surface. Patterns help modulate an overall mood and ambiance. Print Trials, Punch # 2, 1958; Designed by Alexander Hayden Girard (American, 1907–1993); wool (46%) cotton (39%) and rayon (15%); Warp x Weft: 31.1 x 30.5 cm (12 1/4 x 12 in.); Collection of Cooper Hewitt, Smithsonian Design Museum, Gift of Alexander H. Girard; 1969-165-1249, -1239, -1245.

TUMMY TREK To create an educational game about the role of bacteria in the digestive system, designer Yinan Wang used color to convey mood. The game takes place on a river flowing through the large intestine. As food travels down the river, various bacteria aid and hinder the process of digestion. Different color palettes depict the intestinal landscape as a healthy, happy environment (top) or as a gloomy place of intestinal distress (bottom). Design and illustration by Yinan Wang.

Color and Emotion

GOOD MOODS AND BAD MOODS A changing color climate expresses the changing mood of a drama. The storytellers at Pixar Animation Studios create "color scripts" that map out the moods in a film, as expressed through color and lighting.

To create a *color script*, animators apply color to selected frames from the film's storyboard. They create the color script early in the development of a film, providing a high-level representation of the story's emotional arc. According to Pixar, "It's not about making a single pretty piece of art; the color script evolves throughout the early stages of the film, hand in hand with story development."

Designers of games, animations, apps, motion graphics, and other digital experiences can also use color scripts. The palette needs to hang together as a totality, but it can shift and evolve to express dramatic change.

Designers are trained to use colors that delight and inspire. But sometimes we need to stir up some darkness and dread. Well, there's a color for that. A market research firm in Australia has determined that the world's ugliest color is Pantone 448. This drab shade of green resembles a stale cup of coffee tweaked with a squirt of Gatorade. This color was chosen for use on cigarette packages that are designed to be so repulsive, smokers won't want to buy them. The research team asked one thousand smokers to look at an array of awful colors, including mouse gray, lime green, mustard yellow, and basic beige. The color the smokers picked looks a lot like tobacco. This stinky, slimy brown aims to inspire disgust, subverting desire and turning us away. Even worse are the photographs of rotting toes and clogged lungs (consequences of smoking) that also appear on these terrifying packages.

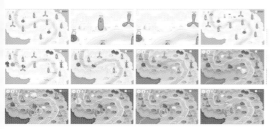

COLOR SCRIPT This tiny storyboard for the game Tummy Trek shows how the shift in color over the course of game play reflects the change from a healthy tummy to a turbulent one. Design and illustration by Yinan Wang.

READ MORE Donald G. McNeil, "How to Get Smokers to Quit? Enlist World's Ugliest Color," *New York Times* (June 20, 2016), https://nyti.ms/2hm5eYl; accessed July 15, 2016; Pixar, "Colour Script," http://pixar-animation.weebly.com/colour-script.html; accessed August 1, 2017.

Perception is a dynamic process. Our senses are driven by action and seek patterns. Our picture of the world at any instant is shaped by what we want to *do*.

Act 3 | Sensation

Illustration by Ellen Lupton

ACT 3

Sensation

Did you ever pull back and imagine your life as a movie? In this cinematic masterpice, you are the filmmaker as well as the featured talent. The process of perception is, indeed, something like making a movie. As your eyes dart about to focus on different people and things, they function a bit like film cameras, combining numerous still pictures to register motion and depth. As we move through space and time, we intuitively predict what will happen next based on previous "frames." (An elephant racing toward you will keep getting bigger.) Cognitive scientists call this filmic sequence of imagery *optic flow*. No single point of focus is ever divorced from what comes immediately before and after.

According to philosopher Alva Noë, "Perception is not something that happens to us, or in us. It is something we do." He explains, for example, why professional baseball players are so good at hitting a tiny ball speeding through the air. They are alert and watching the scene with their whole bodies. A hitter interprets the pitcher's movements and predicts where the ball will go. With the ball moving nearly 100 miles per hour, the hitter has no time to calculate its trajectory or even follow it with his or her eyes. Instead, the batter's body reacts to the precise action of the pitcher in order to almost instantaneously predict the ball's destination.

We tend to see what we are looking for. We don't absorb every detail of an app, a web page, or a crowded room simultaneously. We overlook countless features as we jump around the page or screen, taking focused snapshots in rapid succession. Quick movements of the eye (called *saccades*) allow us to find a price, a headline, a can of soda, or a scary face.

Our optic flow melds with input from other senses. Our "camera angle" changes with each turn of the head. Visual stimuli mix with sound, smell, touch, and the weight and location of bodies in space. Finnish architect Alvar Aalto designed each of his buildings as a flow of physical encounters rather than as a series of static images. Aalto saw a door as an invitation to action—an opportunity to enter, not an abstract rectangle pencilled on a flat plane. The next time you pass through a doorway, notice the sense of compression as the frame of the door pinches the space around your body and then lets you go as the room opens up.

Windows and doors carve passageways through physical space. On a page or screen, boxes, arrows, lines, margins, and frames lead users in and out of content. A poorly designed web page is a patchwork of escape routes and baited traps. Usability expert Jacob Nielsen explains, "On web pages with multiple superfluous images, people treat the entire page as an obstacle course they must navigate."

Like a story, perception is active and temporal. Users of an app or website don't just look, they act. They click, point, scroll, like, and swipe, responding to what they see. All vision involves action and interaction. Vision is a mechanism for perceiving space and time in relation to an observer. This observer has a body—a head that tilts and turns, and hands that reach, touch, and grasp.

Our working memory can hold onto only a few objects at a time. When you actively search for something—from a can of Coke to a lost child—you prime your brain to seek out particular details (a shiny red cylinder or a little blue hoodie). Even when not confronting a specific task, our gaze gravitates toward points of interest, from eyes, mouths, and noses to snakes in the grass and letters on a page. Neuroscientist Jan Lauwereyns explains that perception seeks out a small number of meaningful objects in a sea of stimuli: "preferably important ones, useful or dangerous, beautiful or strange." In a cluttered sign, diagram, or website, noisy distractions overwhelm valuable information.

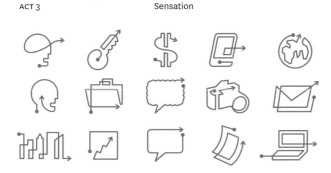

ACTIVE PATH This icon set was designed for the career center at a college. The icons represent the center's range of services. The icons express motion, time, change, and iniative by turning static objects into active paths. Design by PostTypography for MICA.

A product or publication comes to life as people put it to use over time. Anthropologist Tim Ingold has written that landscapes are defined by paths. When people inhabit a place, they cut across it on cleared roads, bodies of water, or swaths of earth beaten down by people and other creatures. Such paths of movement define villages, cities, and roads. Ingold writes, "There can be no places without paths, along which people arrive and depart; and no paths without places." Signs and arrows ease the flow of people through hospitals and airports, while logos and shopwindows promote the flow of capital. A publication or website is a network of passageways and stopping-off points designed to attract and guide attention, to speed it up and slow it down. Any design project is a site of activity, brought to life by the movement of eyes and bodies.

This book invites designers to think about paths, from user journeys to the path of the active, roving eye. Designers use psychological cues to create elements and interfaces that stay in the background, coming forward only when beckoned. Designers also take the eye and body to new places. Much of what we find memorable in a poster, pattern, or page layout involves games of omission, ambiguity, and visual tension. Playful gaps and glitches activate our powers of perception, making us aware of what it means to see.

READ MORE Tim Ingold, "The Temporality of the Landscape," *World Archaeology* 25, no. 2 (October 1993): 152–74; Jan Laureweyns, *Brain and the Gaze* (Cambridge: MIT Press, 2012); Alva Noë, *Action in Perception* (Cambridge: MIT Press, 2004);

Jakob Nielsen and Kara Pernice, *Eye Tracking Web Usability* (London: Pearson Education, Inc. and New Riders, 2010); Juhani Pullasmaa, *The Eyes of the Skin: Architecture and the Senses* (West Sussex, England: Wiley, 2005).

TOOL

The Gaze

Medusa, the famous monster from Greek mythology, was so ugly she turned men into stone if they dared to look at her. Medusa used looking as a tool of destruction. Societies erect rules of behavior about how and when to wield the power of the gaze. Looking downward demonstrates submission and respect; staring or glaring is an act of aggression. Acknowledging the power of the gaze helps designers understand the roving, searching activity of vision. Designers use color and shape, borders and arrows, words and pictures, to attract the gaze of users. Graphic elements captivate the eye or release it to wander along a fluid path.

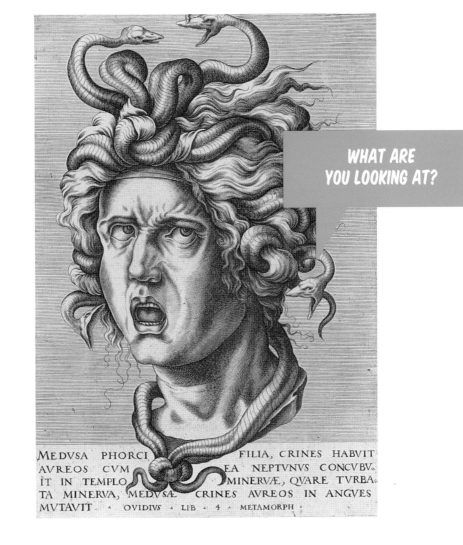

Medusa Head, Anonymous, 1500–1599. Collection of Rijksmuseum, Amsterdam.

The Gaze

THE POWER TO SEE Exploring the world with your eyes is an active process. In every society, some people are more free than others to look or to be looked at.

The gaze is a powerful instrument. To look is to actively search and communicate. We point by directing our gaze at people and objects. "I want that one," you say, casting your gaze at a glossy donut or an enticing dance partner. Wandering through life, we sometimes operate in active search mode—hunting for the bathroom or fumbling for a price tag. At other times, we look around in a more open state, simply taking in our surroundings, receptive to the scene. In either case, our gaze is drawn to points of intrigue, from a dark hole in the middle of the road to a black cat lurking in the shadows. Humans instinctively look for novelty and surprise, because any shift in what we see could be a source of danger or delight.

These visual disruptions mark potential stories embedded in a scene. Change is the basis of narrative, and change motivates the act of looking. Our constant search for change drives the gaze from one point of focus to the next.

Since the birth of advertising, luscious female bodies have been deployed to sell everything from cigarettes to office equipment. A curvy girl draped across a Cadillac makes the car an object of erotic consumption. Looking can be a soothing and seductive source of pleasure. Being looked at, however, can also make people feel excluded from the action or turned into a passive target.

Laura Mulvey's legendary 1975 essay "Visual Pleasure and Narrative Cinema" describes the camera as an extension of the male look, which treats the female body as a sexual object. The audience identifies with the camera and the male gaze. In traditional Hollywood cinema, close-ups of female eyes, lips, and legs flatten women into passive erotic spectacles. The moving camera tends to depict the point of view of the male hero, who dominates the narrative. According to Mulvey, the male protagonist "articulates the look and creates the action."

Mulvey pushed filmmakers to reveal the material presence of the camera and disconnect it from the male gaze. Responding to Mulvey's critique of traditional visual narrative, feminist artists and designers have created alternative representations of women. Putting a gorilla head on a reclining nude delivers a shock to our habits of looking. Gone is the familiar narrative of the passive female body. In the new story that takes its place, women are wild, and they are watching.

In a world structured by sexual imbalance, pleasure in looking has been split between active/male and passive/female.

LAURA MULVEY, "VISUAL PLEASURE AND NARRATIVE CINEMA"

BEHOLD THE GAZE Albrecht Dürer's famous drawing of a draughstman at work (1525) shows a screenlike device for transcribing the scene in two dimensions. Collection of Rijksmuseum, Amsterdam.

READ MORE Jan Lauwereyns, *Brain and the Gaze* (Cambridge: MIT Press, 2012); Laura Mulvey, "Visual Pleasure and Narrative Cinema," 1975, in *Film Theory and Criticism*, ed. Leo Braudy and Marshall Cohen (New York: Oxford University Press, 1999): 833–44.

GUERILLA GIRLS The feminist art collective Guerilla Girls challenges the marginalization of women artists. *Do Women Have to Be Naked to Get into the Met. Museum?* 1989, Offset lithograph, Collection of Cooper Hewitt, Smithsonian Design Museum, Gift of Sara and Marc Benda, 2009-20-2.

The Gaze

EVOLUTION OF THE EYE Biological vision evolved over millions of years, starting with light-sensitive proteins in single-celled organisms. These creatures' ability to sense light developed along with nerve cells enabling the creatures to move and act. These tiny organisms could move toward light to consume energy, or they could hide in darkness to avoid predators.

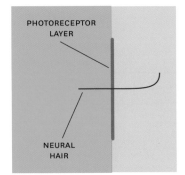

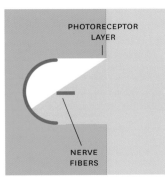

RETINA

OPTIC
NERVE

EUGLENA has a light-sensitive patch and a tiny neural hair. Vision began with light-sensitive patches on single-celled organisms. The microscopic euglena uses a tiny neural hair to travel toward light (to turn it into energy). Over time, organisms evolved who could sense light changing from one instant to the next. Such creatures could thus perceive motion, increasing their ability to find food and avoid danger, and thus enhancing their evolutionary advantage.

PLANARIAN WORM has a dent in its head. The light-sensitive patch of the primitive planarian worm is depressed rather than flat. Light falling on this concave area hits some cells and misses others, because the sides of the dent block the light. (Picture a crater on the moon, with one edge rimmed in shadow.) The planarian worm can thus perceive changes in the direction of light over time, establishing a circadian rhythm or "biological clock" that helps it hide in darkness from predators.

PINHOLE EYE focuses light on a retina. The dent in the head of the nautilus is deeper than that of the planarian worm, forming a spherical cavity with a narrow opening at one end. A beam of light entering this narrow opening focuses light on photoreceptor cells at the back of the cavity (the retina). The cavity thus functions like a biological pinhole camera. The pinhole eye of the nautilus can sense direction and detect shapes with more precision.

Vision supports actions that help creatures survive and reproduce. Vision involves not just sensing light but responding to it.

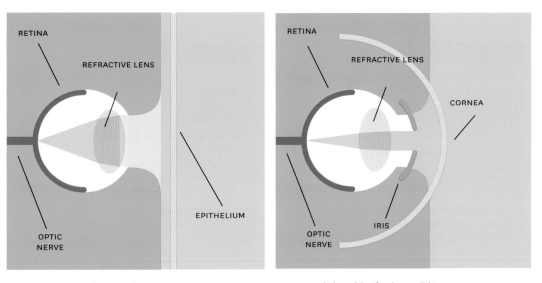

OUTER LENS protects the eye and focuses light. An octopus eye has a thin membrane protecting the fluid-filled interior from infection. A fixed-focus outer lens narrows the beam of light entering the eye. A refractive inner lens enables a wider visual angle and projects a more finely tuned picture on the retina, enabling the eye to focus on objects at varied distances. Depth perception allows an octopus to understand its proximity to desired (or feared) objects.

THE IRIS optimizes vision for day or night. More sophisticated creatures, such as dogs, cats, and people, have a third layer, the iris, that controls how much light enters the eye. The iris narrows in bright light and widens in darkness, enabling creatures to adjust their vision as the environment changes. Anatomical features such as the retina, lens, and iris developed in concert with the brain and optic nerve, allowing creatures to react to their visible surroundings.

Illustrations by Jennifer Tobias

The Gaze

WHERE DOES THE GAZE GO? What do people tend to look at? In what order will they see information? A page packed with texts and images isn't a static composition; it must be traversed over time by the restless eye.

Close your eyes and imagine a man running past you in a purple running suit. Now, think about the picture that just played in your head. Which way was the man running? For many readers of the Latin alphabet, the man in the jogging suit will travel from left to right, like words on a page. Likewise, Latin readers often view images from left to right and top to bottom, the same way we read text. Points of interest, however—such as faces or puppies—will draw our attention away from this general path.

To order a pastry at the donut counter, you point with your eyes as well as your index finger to say, "I want that one." Eyes printed on a package or poster entice viewers to glance back. An image of a face can also direct viewers' attention to whatever the eyes are pointing to.

The Russian scientist Alfred L. Yarbus is the father of modern eye-tracking research. In the 1960s, he attached mirrors and suction cups to the eyeballs of participants to capture their movement. Today's digital eye-tracking technologies continue to study the movement of the thinking eye, exposing behaviors that are hidden from direct consciousness. Made with the help of cameras and computer screens, heat maps and motion diagrams illuminate the involuntary vision patterns of users.

According to vision-tracking research conducted by Jacob Nielsen and Kara Pernice, web users despise advertisments and instinctively skip over them. A person researching the mating habits of mallard ducks will look at pictures of ducks, but not at ads for reducing belly fat. Users tend to avoid pictures that are irrelevant to the subject at hand, as well as images that are poor quality or low contrast. They will also avoid looking at generic stock photos. People want to look at real ducks, not ducks posing at a corporate picnic.

Designers can use such research insights to please and delight users instead of junking up the visual field. The competition for human attention has often been called a "battle for eyeballs." It's useful to know that the eyeball is not a mindless optical machine. It has learned to repel—with ruthless precision—the aresenal of visual crap strewn in its path.

TRACKING THE GAZE To conduct his eye-tracking research, Soviet scientist Alfred L. Yarbus immobilized his subjects' heads and taped open their eyes. He attached a contraption made of lights and mirrors to the eyeball with a suction cup. The mirrors beamed light onto photosenstive paper. The research subjects thus created drawings with their eyeballs, recording the staccato path of the human gaze. When shown the face of a young girl, the eye gravitated to the girls' eyes and mouth, natural points of interest. Alfred L. Yarbus, *Eye Movements and Vision* (New York: Plenum Press, 1967); Jakob Nielsen and Kara Pernice, *Eye Tracking Web Usability* (London: Pearson Education, Inc. and New Riders, 2010).

HOW DO YOU READ A PICTURE? In the illustration of the scary doctor, our gaze tends to gravitate to his eyes first and then to the ominous needle on the left side of the image. Having set up the archetype of the evil doctor and his wicked tools, the artist now breaks expectations and shows us a menacing bank check. The scariest thing about medicine is not the procedure but paying the bill! Christoph Niemann, a designer, illustrator, and author working in Berlin, has built a career creating surprising narrative pictures like this one.

His visual stories often have a beginning, middle, and end (doctor, needle, shocking price tag), even when the story is told in a single frame. The black and red illustrations above read from top to bottom. Here, Niemann sets up an expetaction at the top of the picture (knitting a sweater or hanging laundry). The punchline arrives at the bottom, upsetting our intitial assumptions. Illustrations by Christoph Niemann.

TOOL
Gestalt Principles

Look around and notice how objects emerge from other objects. Millions of hairs on your dog's back and thousands of tufts of fiber sprouting from the rug melt together to become a sleeping canine or a shaggy carpet. According to the **Gestalt principles** of perception, the brain converts a flood of data about color, tone, shape, movement, and orientation into distinct objects. These useful chunks of information are called *percepts*. A cluster of dots becomes a face. A clump of letters becomes a word. Dashes painted on a roadway define a path. Designers produce forms that stand out against the clutter of experience or pull away into the background.

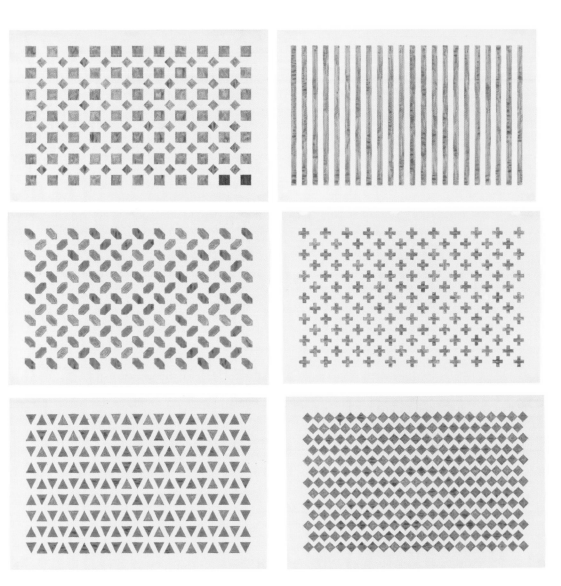

NAPKIN SKETCHES Alexander Hayden Girard was a prolific designer of furniture, textiles, and interiors. Shown here are drawings he created for dinner napkins for a restaurant he designed in 1959. Each pattern stimulates and activates the eye. The spaces between elements undulate from figure to ground, as shapes group into dynamic stripes and diagonals.

Drawings, Napkin Designs for La Fonda del Sol Restaurant, ca. 1959; Designed by Alexander Hayden Girard (American, 1907–1993); USA; brush and watercolor on blueprint grid on white wove paper; 40.6 x 61cm (16 x 24in.); Collection of Cooper Hewitt, Smithsonian Design Museum, Gift of Alexander H. Girard; 1969-165-334, -324, -327, -331, -333, -335.

Gestalt Principles

PARTS AND WHOLES German psychologists in the early twentieth century studied the active character of vision. They founded the Gestalt theory of perception, which explores how the brain groups elements into larger wholes.

Gestalt psychologist Max Wertheimer wrote, "The whole is different from the sum of its parts." In a map or diagram, elements grouped by size, shape, or color become distinct layers of information. In a field of text, letters group into words, lines, and columns. In an icon system, images take shape from geometric elements. In a patterned textile, repeated parts create a rhythmic surface. By playing with relationships between parts and wholes, designers make images come alive in peoples' minds.

Grouping is inherently active, allowing viewers to move between contradictory understandings of an object or element. A dot, dash, or letter is a single particle; at the same time it belongs to a continuous line or a larger field. Calling attention to the conflict between parts and wholes prompts mental work from viewers, foregrounding perception as a dynamic experience.

According to the Gestalt principle of *simplicity*, the brain groups elements in order to minimize the number of objects in a scene. Pursuing simplicity became an aesthetic imperative for modern designers.

Grouping underlies our perception of complex scenes in the living environment as well as two-dimensional patterns and surfaces. The Gestalt principle of *common fate* holds that items moving or changing simultaneously will form a group. A lion blends into the grass, camouflaged by its surroundings. As the lion leaps into action, she separates from the background. The common fate of her contour provides a life-or-death signal to potential prey. Figure/ground is the process of separating a dominant element from its surroundings. In a pattern of uniform stripes or checkerboard squares, the relationship between figure and ground is shifting and ambiguous.

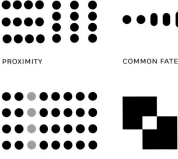

PROXIMITY

COMMON FATE

CLOSURE   SYMMETRY

SIMILARITY

FIGURE/GROUND AMBIGUITY

CONTINUATION

GESTALT PRINCIPLES

PROXIMITY Closely spaced elements form groups.

SIMILARITY Elements with the same color or shape are a group.

COMMON FATE Elements appear to change as a group.

FIGURE/GROUND AMBIGUITY White spaces can read either as foreground or background.

CLOSURE AND CONTINUATION We mentally close the gaps in the regular shapes or strong lines.

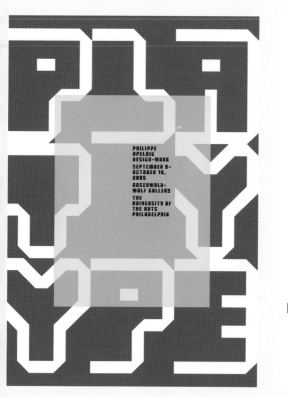

ACTIVE VISION These posters and letterforms, designed by Philippe Apeloig, invite viewers to experience vision as an active process. The principles of proximity, continuation, and closure come into play as viewers spontaneously build wholes out of parts, fill in the gaps between elements, and see white spaces oscillate between figure and ground. This process of witnessing visual conflicts and contradictions yields surprise and delight. Clockwise from upper left: Play Type, poster for an exhibition at the Rosenwald-Wolf Gallery, The University of the Arts, Philadelphia; Xtra Train, poster celebrating the 70th anniversary of the National Railways of France; the letter "Z" from nine typefaces designed by Philippe Apeloig: Coupé Regular, Ali, Octobre, Abf Linéaire Regular, Poudre One, Abf Petit, Ndebele Plain, Abf Silhouette, Izocel; typefaces available from Nouvelle Noir type foundry, Switzerland, https://nouvellenoire.ch. Design by Philippe Apeloig.

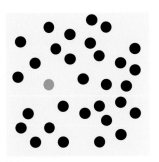

Color

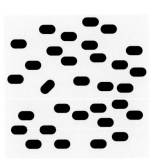

Orientation

Scale

Motion

HUNGRY FOR DIFFERENCE The gaze constantly seeks new information. We quickly perceive anomalies in the visual field. Designers use changes in color, size, orientation, and motion to make an element easy to find.

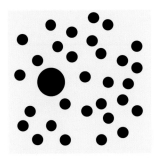

The upside-down M is harder to find than the bold M.

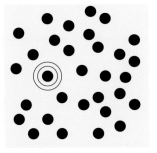

The flipped K is harder to find than the K that's filled in.

EASY AND HARD Some differences are easier to see than others. Each of these diagrams includes one unique character that stands out from the crowd and another unique character that more or less blends in. Designers create various relationships of difference and similarity when they work with data, typography, patterns, textures, and other applications.

The light green Z is harder to find than the orange Z.

The L is harder to find than the plus sign.

Illustrations by Jennifer Tobias; adapted from Colin Ware, *Visual Thinking for Design* (Burlington, MA: Elsevier, 2008).

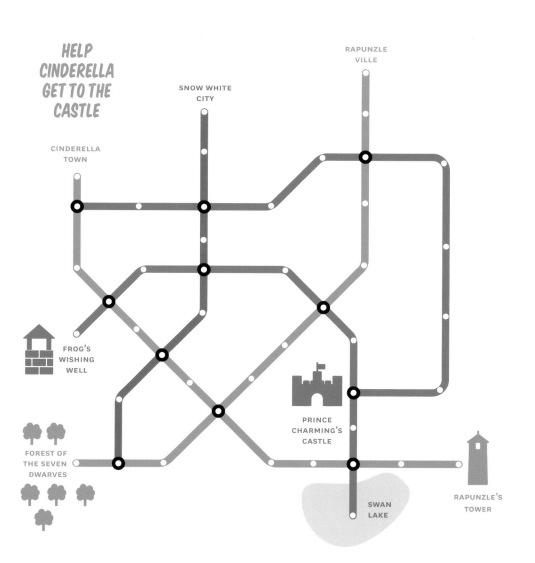

HELP CINDERELLA GET TO THE CASTLE

RAPUNZLE VILLE

SNOW WHITE CITY

CINDERELLA TOWN

FROG'S WISHING WELL

PRINCE CHARMING'S CASTLE

FOREST OF THE SEVEN DWARVES

SWAN LAKE

RAPUNZLE'S TOWER

NETWORK MAP If Cinderella takes the wrong route, she will end up at Rapunzel's Tower instead of Prince Charming's Castle. Her powers of perception will help her find the right path. Color unifies each of the five train lines (continuation). The large black dots are easy to find and read as a separate plane (similarity). Designers use perceptual principles to create information graphics that are intuitive to read.

READ MORE Johan Wagemans, James H. Elder, Michael Kubovy, Stephen E. Palmer, Mary A. Peterson, Manish Singh, and Rüdiger von der Heydt, "A Century of Gestalt Psychology in Visual Perception, I. Perceptual Grouping and Figure-Ground Organization," *Psychological Bulletin* 138, no. 6 (November 2012): 1172–1217, doi:10.1037/a0029333.

TOOL
Affordance

Action is the essence of storytelling. Designers create cues and pathways that guide the actions of users. Buttons are for pushing, menus are for scrolling, and the pages of a book are for flipping, turning, and marking. An object that triggers an action is called an affordance. Some affordances are accidental: a window ledge near a bus stop is a handy place to rest a coffee cup. Many responses to affordances are instinctive. A high cliff affords falling, so people and other creatures stay away from the edge. Other affordances are learned over time. The bars, buttons, and menus on a website or an app borrow imagery from physical objects. Shadows and highlights make these digital fictions seem more physically real—and they invite action from users.

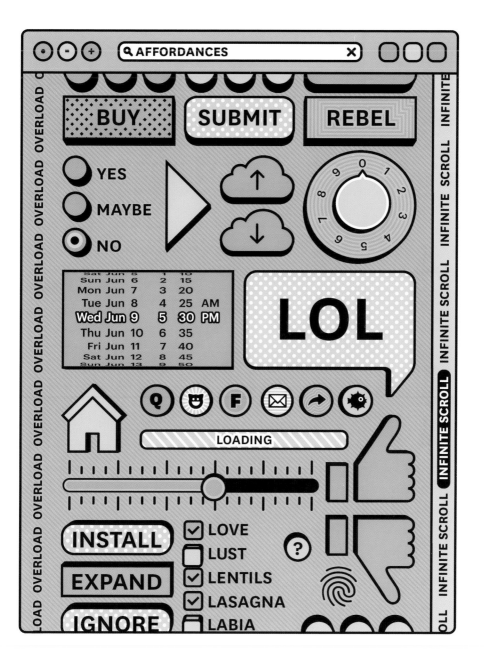

Illustration by Jason Gottlieb

AFFORDANCES—
THE MANUAL TYPEWRITER

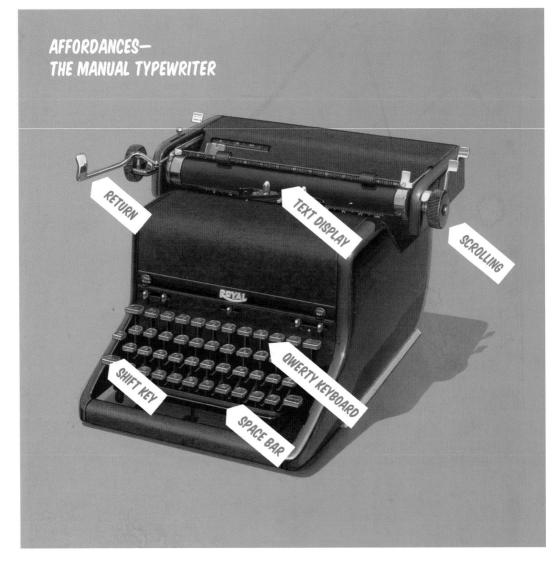

RETURN

TEXT DISPLAY

SCROLLING

SHIFT KEY

QWERTY KEYBOARD

SPACE BAR

PHYSICAL AFFORDANCES Mechanical controls such as levers, buttons, and wheels are examples of affordances. Their shape, position, familiarity, and graphic markings invite action from users. The typewriter shown here was designed by Henry Dreyfuss in 1944. His design philosophy sought to fit "the machine to the man rather than the man to the machine." Dreyfuss's design preserved features of typewriters that had already been standard for over fifty years, including a cylindrical rubber carriage with a wheel for advancing a sheet of paper up and down, and a lever for finishing a line and advancing

the paper the distance required to begin a new line. While many earlier typewriter designs exposed the inner workings of the machine, Dreyfuss and other modern designers preferred to reveal only those parts of the machine that people would interact with. Many devices today adhere to this principle. Drawing, Design for Royal Typewriter, 1944; Designed by Henry Dreyfuss (American, 1904–1972); USA; gouache, pen and black ink, white chalk, graphite on cream illustration board; 46.4 x 35.9 cm (18 1/4 x 14 1/8 in.); Collection of Cooper Hewitt, Smithsonian Design Museum; Gift of John Bruce; 1993-65-1.

AFFORDANCES— THE SMARTPHONE

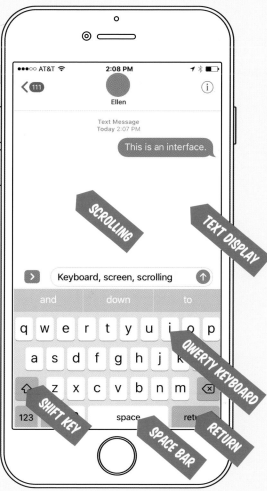

DIGITAL AFFORDANCES The text messaging interface shown here includes a keyboard and a scrolling display. Subtle shadows recall physical keys that can be handled and touched. The first six keys in the top row spell out the word "QWERTY." Back in the early days of mechanical typewriters, the peculiar arrangement of the QWERTY keyboard was believed to prevent keys from jamming by slowing typists down. If a typist was working too fast, the keys could fly up and hit the paper at nearly the same time, creating a tangled mess. Thus the QWERTY keyboard was explicitly designed to prevent optimal performance.

Long after such mechanical problems were eliminated, the QWERTY layout stayed in use. Once you have learned to type using this layout, it is difficult to unlearn it and embrace a new one—even though today's devices bear no technical resemblance to their forebears. Despite many efforts at reform, generations of typists have been stuck with this illogical affordance. A smartphone has various physical affordances not found on mechanical typewriters, from the home button to the camera and volume controls, as well as numerous digital affordances that have become new standards.

Affordances

JUST-IN-TIME REPRESENTATION Try this visual test. Look at the icons on the facing page and find the Twitter logo. You may stumble on an eagle or a paper airplane before finding what you are looking for, but you probably hit your target in a second or two.

When searching for something specific—such as a car in a parking lot or a friend's face in a crowd—people actively focus on the task at hand, sifting out irrelevant details. Vision is an active, goal-oriented activity that reserves attention for valued information. The designers of the Twitter logo used distinctive graphics to create a brand identity you can quickly find and act on.

Try the same experiment with the word "dog," which is written somewhere in the following paragraphs. You might stumble on a few false positives along the way ("fog" or "dot"), but despite the hazards, you can quickly find what you are looking for. You draw on your powers of perception and your familiarity with reading and typography to finish the job efficiently.

Computer scientist Dana Harry Ballard calls this process *just-in-time representation*. Ballard is the creator of computerized machines that simulate human vision. In 1985, he helped build a robotic camera that moves rapidly about like the human eye. In fields ranging from cognitive science to artificial intelligence, scientists are modelling vision in order to help computers find meaning in what they see.

Immersed in a fog of competing signals, we simplify what we see in order to distinguish earth from sky, objects from backgrounds, motion from stillness, dashes from dots. Whether searching for the letters *d-o-g* printed on a page or looking for a lost poodle in a busy park, we ignore non-essential stimuli. If a rabid dog suddenly rushed into your visual field, your whole body would react. Your arms would fly up to protect your face. Your shoulders would twist defensively, and you would crouch down to enable leaping out of the way. Sensory details less essential to your immediate survival—such as a plastic bag impaled in a tree or a mosquito biting your neck—would go unnoticed.

Just-in-time representation is a useful phenomenon to keep in mind when designing a simple logo or a complex map. How will users find your symbol in the crowd? How will they make their way through layers of data? Creating strong shapes and clear links and separations among elements helps users find meaning and make sense of the visual field.

Biological vision gears its computational activity closely and sparingly to the task at hand, making the most efficient use of the persisting external scene. ANDY CLARK

HOW FAST CAN YOU FIND
THE TWITTER LOGO?

FIND IT JUST IN TIME To locate the Twitter logo, you didn't test each image one by one. When the brain is primed to search for particular objects, signs, or colors, we quickly find what we are looking for and ignore the rest. Illustration by Yi Pan.

TOOL

Behavioral Economics

Humans constantly make decisions based on impulses, gut feelings, or force of habit. Such decisions evade rational analysis. Making a choice quickly helps us get through life. If a person decided to do a cost/benefit analysis before choosing a seat on the bus or deciding which article to read first on a news site, they would have a slow time getting through the day. **Behavioral economics** studies human decision making. Design elements such as size and color often provide the extra push or "nudge" that gets someone to click a link or choose a product. Although blinking buttons and shiny graphics can be used for nefarious purposes, designers can apply insights about human behavior for social benefit.

WHICH DETERGENT WOULD YOU RATHER USE?

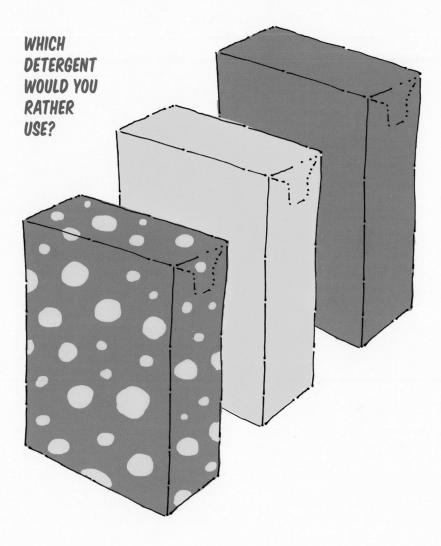

BOX STORY Participants in a study were given three boxes of detergent to test over a period of time. The detergent inside the boxes was all the same, but the packages were printed in different colors: some were blue, some were yellow, and some were both blue and yellow. Users generally preferred the detergent in the multicolored boxes, yet they didn't report this to the researchers. They explained their choices in terms of the product's performance, but in fact, the only real difference was graphic design. Illustration by Jennifer Tobias.

Behavioral Economics

ART OF THE NUDGE Seemingly minor design decisions—like preselecting a radio button or changing the color of a candy wrapper—can influence choices at an unconscious level. Behavioral economists show how such design elements affect people's decisions.

When faced with a choice between three different service plans or three different smartphones, many people will pick the middle option. They feel instinctively that the cheaper one isn't good enough and the most expensive one is too extravagant. Thus marketing professionals carefully design the pricing and features of different plans and products, knowing that the middle one will be the most popular—and the choices on either side will make it even more so.

People also tend to accept defaults. Consider the problem of how to increase the number of organ donors. In many nations, citizens automatically become donors when they register for driver's licenses. These citizens can easily opt out, but the vast majority don't. In the United States, citizens must explicitly opt *in* to become organ donors. Faced with making the decision more actively, people are more likely to become skeptical and suspicious, rejecting this safe, hugely beneficial, lifesaving program.

In the United States and other countries around the world, portion sizes have ballooned as the cost of industrially produced food has dropped. Rising rates of obesity and diabetes accompany those giant plates of pasta and super-sized sodas. Research shows that people eat more when a bigger portion appears to be normal. Consumption goes up when there's a huge spoon in the candy dish or when a giant bag of chips costs a penny more than a tiny one.

Using this knowledge, Brian Wansink, founder of the Food and Brand Lab at Cornell University, pushed food producers to create 100-calorie snack packs. His lab also found that people will eat more jelly beans when many colors are mixed together than when the colors are sorted into separate containers, because people believe that varied foods taste better. M&M candies all taste the same—regardless of color—but people will eat fewer M&Ms if all the candies in the bowl are one hue. Verbal descriptions such as "farm-fresh eggs" or "baby garden lettuce" influence not only which items people choose but their perceptions of how good they taste.

Designers must proceed with caution when applying insights from behavioral economics and other fields of psychology. The practice of presenting pre-checked boxes on a website or tricking users into spamming their contact list are examples of "dark patterns." It is unethical to trick someone into buying insurance they don't want or supporting a cause they disagree with. Common dark patterns include disguising advertisements as editorial content ("click bait") and making it difficult for users to disable a feature or cancel a subscription (called a "roach motel").

Like doctors, designers should pledge to do no harm and use the amazing power of language and design to advance the common good.

Environmental factors have a powerful—and unconscious—influence not only on how much we eat but on how food tastes. LEONARD MLODINOW

WHICH
POPCORN
WOULD YOU
RATHER
EAT?

STALE!

FRESH!

TASTE TEST Various studies have shown that portion sizes—not just natural appetite—influence how much food people eat. In one experiment, participants outside a movie theater were offered boxes of popcorn. Both portions were beyond what a person might normally eat, but one was smaller than the other. The large box was filled with stale popcorn, and the smaller one with fresh popcorn. Participants tended to eat more food from the bigger container, despite its crappy contents. Illustration by Jennifer Tobias.

READ MORE Harry Brignall, DarkPatterns.org, accessed July 28, 2017; Daniel Kahneman, *Thinking, Fast and Slow* (New York: Farrar, Straus and Giroux, 2015); Leonard Mlodinow, *Subliminal: How the Unconscious Mind Rules Your Behavior* (New York: Vintage Books, 2012); Richard Thaler, Cass R. Sunstein, and Sean Pratt, *Nudge: Improving Decisions about Health, Wealth, and Happiness* (London: Penguin Books, 2009); Brian Wansink, *Mindless Eating: Why We Eat More Than We Think* (London: Hay House, 2011).

TOOL

Multisensory Design

Reaching beyond design's traditional focus on vision, **multisensory design** incorporates the full range of bodily experience. We experience the world with all our senses, using data about the environment to move around, avoid danger, and communicate with others. Drinking a cup of coffee involves multiple senses. The brain combines input about taste, smell, temperature, and texture to create "flavor." The chair supporting your back, the sun drifting through the windows, and the music whispering from the speakers also affect your experience. Language makes an impact, too. Is that just a plain old cup of coffee, or is it Finca El Puente with plum notes and a toasted nut finish?

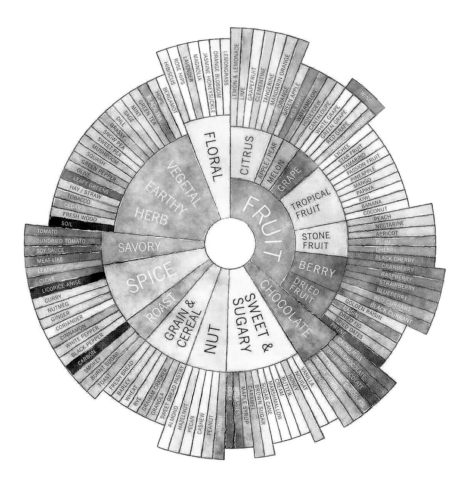

SENSORY COLOR PALETTE In this chart published by Counter Culture Coffee, the larger flavor wedges represent categories more commonly used by tasters, such as citrus, berry, and chocolate. CCC plans to update the wheel as coffee preferences change as well as publish different versions for different regions of the world. The language of taste and smell is regional and subjective. Design by Tim Hill.

Multisensory Design

DIMMER SWITCH Try taking a shower in the dark. For a sighted person, this will be a disorienting experience. You may struggle to adjust the water temperature or to find the right soap, but you will learn about the importance of multisensory design.

Next time you take a shower, pay attention to non-visual feedback. What happens when you grasp the faucet, squeeze a soap bottle, or lather your head with a scented brew of glycol and glycerin? Designers have worked hard to orchestrate your in-shower experience. Industrial designers and engineers have crafted the feel of the faucet and the resistance it offers as you turn the knob. Package designers have used flexible plastic to make your shampoo bottles soft to touch, and they have devised hinged lids that flip open so the caps don't fall off and get lost. Scent designers have given the soap inside the bottle its gentle fragrance or invigorating aroma.

Notice how textures, shapes, and smells connect with visible features. Does the shape of your shower hardware underscore its rotational movement? Does the color of the shampoo bottle enhance your sensory impressions? Does the conditioner's milky richness promise to nourish your scalp, repair split ends, or save the planet? Does the product's name make you think of shady gardens or tropical cocktails? Shampoo does more than strip the grit and grease from your hair: it draws on multiple sensations to make a daily ritual more pleasing and convenient.

If you are blind or visually impaired, your experience in the shower will be different from that of a sighted person. Your sense of touch, smell, and sound will provide crucial information for completing everyday tasks safely and confidently. People with dementia may rely on stronger differences among products to avoid getting confused, while people with autism spectrum disorder (ASD) could be overwhelmed by soap that smells too strong or water that is too hot or loud.

Design researcher Deana McDonagh is an advocate for empathic design. By exploring a city or classroom while wearing earplugs or a blindfold, designers with normal hearing or vision can build empathy and learn the importance of multisensory design elements. She suggests that designers collaborate with people with disabilities, working with them as peers and life experts. Designers should step back throughout their process and consider how people with different abilities might experience a given solution. In digital design, clear guidelines have been established to insure universal solutions. Packaging and product interfaces should be designed so that people can interact with them not just visually, but by touch.

DO IT IN THE DARK Students at MICA (Maryland Institute College of Art) took showers in the dark and observed their experiences. One student slipped and fell. Another pulled the shower control out of the wall and dropped it on his foot. Several students left the curtain at half-mast and got water all over the floor. In addition to making mistakes, however, the designers activated their non-visual intelligence. One found herself using her feet as well as her hands to gather tactile information about the edges of the space. Others felt heightened awareness of the smell, silkiness, and even sound of different products. Illustrations by Jennifer Tobias.

READ MORE Deana McDonagh, "Design Students Forseeing the Unforeseeable: Practice-based Empathic Research Methods," *International Journal of Education through Art*, 11, no. 3 (2015), doi:10.1386/eta.11.3.421_1.

WHICH PACKAGES WORK BETTER IN THE DARK?

SAME

These containers for shampoo and conditioner
have the same shape, color, and typography.

DIFFERENT

These containers for shampoo and conditioner
are different shapes, so it's easy to tell them apart.

DIFFERENT

These containers for shampoo and conditioner
have different textures and caps with different shapes.
The color of the products inside have different intensities.

ONE PUMP, ONE PRODUCT

Combining shampoo and conditioner into a single product
eliminates the need for different packages altogether. The pump
dispenser makes portion control easy without looking.

HOT COFFEE Imagine two cups of carryout coffee. One is from Starbucks, and the other is from Dunkin' Donuts. One cup is made of paper, and the other is Styrofoam. Each cup tells a story about flavor, function, and value.

The Starbucks cup has your name written on it in black Sharpie. It is wrapped in a loose cardboard sleeve to protect your skin from the scalding beverage inside. The Dunkin' Donuts cup feels cooler to touch. As you lift each one to drink, its weight tells you how much coffee is left. The foam cup feels thicker and more porous against your lips than the lightly waxed rim of paper, and the Styrofoam has a plastic taste.

Each cup is a vessel of communication as well as coffee, speaking about the place that sells it and the people who use it. Starbucks provides upscale goods at a premium price, while Dunkin' Donuts promotes low cost and convenience. Each cup communicates with physical interaction as well as logos and graphics. Full or empty, warm or cool, paper or plastic: a cup of coffee reminds us that life is short and its pleasures rich.

A sturdy drawing of a wide-brimmed cup appears in many of the Dunkin' Donuts' signs and advertisements. The curly lines rising from the open cup suggest both heat and aroma. The graphic cup is a vital sidekick to DD's chubby pink-and-orange logotype. Dunkin' Donuts has successfully applied its donut-centric brand to a wide range of sandwiches, snacks, and beverages. Dunkin' Donuts' cool-to-touch Styrofoam cup is a symbol of this popular, affordable brand. Yet the big foam cup may soon drift into cultural memory. In 2015 the company began phasing out Styrofoam and searching for a more sustainable solution, such as doubling up paper cups or using polystyrene, a harder, slicker plastic that can be recycled. The iconic drawing of the cup remains part of the company's image even as the thing itself gets harder to find.

PAPER OR PLASTIC Which cup of coffee is more personal? Which feels better in your hand? Which tastes better when it reaches your mouth? Which costs more? Which is a better value? Materials and touch contribute to our experience of flavor and our memories and beliefs about brands. The rounded shapes of the Dunkin' Donuts logo, designed in 1975 by Lucia DeRespinas, aptly visualize the sweet, doughy richness of the brand's signature pastry product. The green Starbucks logo conveys a more natural vibe. Illustration by Jennifer Tobias.

UNSWELLOWED POWDERED MEDICINE
CHEWING A CARROT AFTER DRINKING COFFEE
BURNED BREAD
DANDELION GREENS
THE FIRST TASTE OF COFFEE
EYE DROPS RUNNING DOWN A THROAT
THE REMAINING AFTER SHAVE ON THE FACE
A MEMORY OF DEFEAT
CITRUS PEEL
RED GINSENG EXTRACT TEA
ORANGE JUICE AFTER BRUSHING TEETH

MORNING AFTER HEAVY DRINKING
AN UNRIPE PEACH
FLAT ENGLISH PALE ALE
INSECTS ENTERING THE MOUTH
A ROOT OF A TREE
BILE JUICE
99% CACAO CHOCOLATE
CHEWING CINNAMON STICKS
BRUSH TEETH AND DRINK ORANGE JUICE
TIRED CYCLISTS SIT WITH BEER

A NYC STREET VENDOR PRETZEL
ANYTHING WITH FETA
ANCHOVIES
THE LAST POTATO CHIP
HAMBURGER WITH PLENTY OF KETCHUP
BUFFALO CHICKEN WINGS WATCHING FOOTBALL GAMES
FISHERMAN'S HANDS
A BIG MOUTHFUL OF CAVIAR
CURED OLIVES
NACHOS WITH SALSA AND CHEESE
SWEAT AFTER HARD WORK
RAMEN WITH A SMALL AMOUNT OF WATER
TEARS OF SORROW
SUSHI DUNKED INTO SOY SAUCE
RUNNY NOSE
MOVIE THEATER POPCORN
LONG BOILED CHICKEN NOODLE SOUP
CRISPY BACON IN CARBONARA

TASTY TYPE Dunkin Donuts' and other food brands have used typography to emulate taste and texture. Smoothy King, purveyor of icy fruit-based shakes, has a logo that looks like a melting crown. Seeking a more experimental approach, designer Ann Sunwoo interviewed people about their reactions to basic tastes: sweet, sour, salty, and bitter. She interpreted their responses by creating typefaces with related characteristics. She also chose colors and textures to complement each taste. Design by Ann Sunwoo.

READ MORE Sarah Hyndman, *The Type Taster: How Fonts Influence You* (UK: Type Tasting, 2015).

Multisensory Design

COLOR AND FLAVOR Color makes ice cream taste sweeter, veggies taste fresher, and coffee taste richer. This phenomenon isn't false or misleading—it's the stuff of lived experience, the everyday reality of how our senses intermix.

Every time you eat a jellybean, you consume a representation. That juicy hue primes your expectations about flavor. Try eating one with your eyes closed. Without color, you might be hard-pressed to tell lemon from lime (or from strawberry or raspberry, for that matter). The hyped-up hue of a jellybean magnifies the hint of flavor hiding beneath the heavy cloak of sweetness.

The sourness of lemon is an aspect of its taste. Sensors on the tongue pick up five basic tastes: sweet, sour, salty, bitter, and umami (the Japanese word for deliciousness). In addition to sensing these five basic tastes, humans can process millions of different aromas, transmitted to the brain by olfactory nerves located in the nasal cavity. Without aroma, lemon and lime lack the floral, woodsy notes that come from their unique botanical makeups. The full phenomenon of flavor also includes "mouth-feel" (the crunch of a corn chip and the slippery goodness of guacamole) and chemosensory responses (the heat of cayenne and the coolness of mint).

Color plays a big role in our experience of flavor. In a 2004 study of the relationship between color and scent, participants were asked to smell familiar odors with and without the presence of a supporting color. Yellow boosted the brain's response to the smell of lemons, while brown increased the response to caramel. These effects were measured with fMRI scans while the subjects rated the intensity of the scents.

What can designers learn from studies like this? Changing the intensity of a color on a package, fabric, room color, or interface element can intensify the content or emotional value of the product or place. Colors have strong associations with food and flavor, and different foods carry different associations of mood and setting. Delivered in the context of words, images, activities, and other cues, a color palette recalling tropical fruit or fresh herbs could influence the response of users. Many designs for food brands include a range of colors designed to suggest flavor variations. Different types of tea, such as oolong, Earl Grey, and English Breakfast, look similar when you drink them but have different flavors. Colored packaging helps consumers remember how different teas taste.

Packaging systems for everything from chocolate and vinegar to dish soap and shampoo graft distinctive color palettes onto flavors and scents. Even a product line with little variation of taste or smell can use color to invoke subtle sensory differences. Brands of milk graded from zero fat to full fat use color as a memory cue, even though these products smell the same; only their texture registers a slight difference in mouthfeel. Designers can use hues that suggest the smell of flowers or the taste of candy to bring a sensual dimension to products that are digital or environmental, from the buttons on an app to the fabrics on furniture.

READ MORE H.A. Roth et al, "Psychological relationships between perceived sweetness and color in lemon- and lime-flavored drinks," *Journal of Food Science* 53 (1988): 1116–1119; M. Zampini et al, "The Multisensory Perception of Flavor: Assessing the Influence of Color Cues on Flavor Discrimination Responses," *Food Quality and Preference* 18, no. 7: 975–84, 2007.

WHICH DRINK TASTES SWEETER?

WHICH DRINK TASTES LIKE STRAWBERRIES?

TASTE TEST Try these experiments on some willing human subjects. Add food coloring to a sweet, colorless soda such as Sprite. Does the soda taste sweeter or more flavorful as the color intensifies? Does the flavor change if you change the color? Illustrations by Jennifer Tobias.

ADOBE ILLUSTRATOR FOOD AND BEVERAGE PALETTE

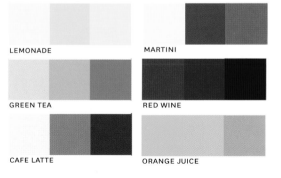

LEMONADE   MARTINI   URINE

GREEN TEA   RED WINE   VOMIT

CAFE LATTE   ORANGE JUICE   DOG FARTS

LANGUAGE MATTERS Colors named after appealing foods and beverages reinforce connections between color and taste. Giving the colors a different name changes the story.

WHITE WINE TASTES LIKE	*RED WINE TASTES LIKE*
LEMON	CHICKORY
GRAPEFRUIT	PEONY
STRAW	PRUNE
BANANA	BLUEBERRY
LYCHEE	RASPBERRY
SULFUR	CLOVE
BOXTREE	CHERRY
PEANUT	STRAWBERRY
MANGO	CEDAR
MELON	MUSK
LIME TREE	HAVANA
BUTTER	CHOCOLATE
WHITE PEACH	VIOLET
YELLOW PEACH	COCOA
QUINCE	BLACK CURRANT
CITRUS FRUIT	TOBACCO
APRICOT	CINNAMON
ALMOND	RED CURRANT
FLOWER	COAL
PEAR	TAR

Multisensory Design

Red or White? Wine tasters use metaphors to describe aroma. In a famous research study, expert tasters tended to compare white wine to pale elements—such as lemon or straw—while comparing red wine to dark elements—such as prune and cocoa.

Do you think you could tell white wine from red wine if you couldn't see their colors? The task is not as easy as you might guess. Wine connoisseurs use language to describe the aromas of wine. Some of these words are shared among communities of tasters and other are developed over time by individual experts, but these vocabularies share a striking feature: the words describing white wines mostly refer to pale or yellow sources (white peach, citrus, straw), while the words describing red wines favor red or deep-hued objects (tobacco, carbon, raspberry). Considered rationally, flavor has no inherent color—a taste or aroma consists of molecules picked up by receptors on the tongue or in the nose. Evaluating taste and smell is not a rational matter, however. We make strong emotional connections between smells, flavors, and colors. We use metaphors to communicate our responses, such as comparing the delicate aromas in a glass of white wine to the aromas (and colors) of mango and straw.

In 2001, French scientists Gil Morrot, Frédéric Brochet, and Denis Dubourdieu studied the influence of color words on wine tasting. They conducted a series of experiments with fifty-four wine experts. First, they asked participants to compare the aromas of two wines, one red and one white, using a list of words drawn from established wine-tasting sources. Participants could also use their own words.

In a second session, participants once again described two wines. They didn't know, however, that these were the same wines from the first session—and one of them had been colored red. Participants were asked to describe the aroma of the two wines with words they had chosen in the first session, including words they had introduced themselves. The results were astonishing. Overwhelmingly, participants used red-wine colors to describe the white wine that had been dyed red, and they tended to eliminate descriptors used in round one that refer to light or yellow sources.

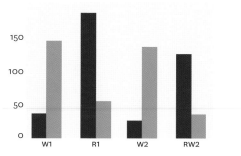

COLOR TEST In a wine-tasting study, most of the terms participants used to describe the aromas of white wine refer to pale or yellowish objects (W1). When the same wine was colored red (RW2), participants described it mostly with words referring to dark or reddish objects. Adapted from Gil Morrot, Frédéric Brochet, and Denis Dubourdieu, "The Color of Odors," *Brain and Language* (2001), doi:10.1006/brln.2001.2493. Illustration by Jennifer Tobias.

[Curtains close, and house lights come up. Search the area for personal belongings.]

Aftermath

Improve Your Writing

LANGUAGE LESSONS Jed Jecelin, a copywriter for the global sportswear maker Under Armour, tells a story about writing web text for a company-sponsored event. The CEO marched angrily into the Jecelin's office and said, "Read me the second sentence on the registration page."

Jecelin wondered what could possibly be wrong with the very basic prose he had written. Worried, he began to read the text out loud to his boss: "*If you would like to participate. . .*"

"Stop right there," snapped the CEO. "At Under Armour we never use the word *participate*. We say *compete*." Language expresses personality and point of view. "Participate" sounds friendly and inclusive, while "compete" suggests relentless drive and energy. One word works for the brand; the other one doesn't.

Words are everywhere in design practice. Products have names. Buildings have signs. Websites have registration pages. A pitch or presentation requires a deck loaded with clear, snappy text. From headlines and micro-copy to instructions and FAQs, well-written copy shapes an emotional response. Would you rather attend a workshop called "Optimizing Community-Based Impact for Youth Organizers" or "Social Action for Young Adults"? Good writing welcomes an audience and sets a tone.

Every sentence tells a story. Every sentence has a hero and an action. A sentence can sizzle with suspense or wilt with fatigue. The following tips and techniques will help you improve your writing as well as to prepare effective presentations and public talks.

READ MORE Steven Pinker, *The Sense of Style: The Thinking Person's Guide to Writing in the 21st Century* (London: UK Allen Lane, 2014); William Knowlton Zinsser, *On Writing Well: The Classic Guide to Writing Nonfiction* (New York: Morrow Quill, 1976).

But wait, I'm scared. I have writer's block!

● Instead of struggling to compose a brilliant first sentence, list the main points you want to make. Don't worry about the order.
● Go back and group your points into sections. A pitch or presentation should have three to five main sections.
● If making a list feels too linear, create a word map instead. Write your main idea in a bubble in the middle of a sheet of paper. Draw more bubbles with points and subpoints.
● Do research. Gathering evidence will help you create compelling content. It will also help you defeat writer's block.

I have notes and a general plan. Now what?

● Start writing in a relaxed, conversational way. Focus on the content, not the words, as if you were speaking to someone. Later, you can improve the writing style.
● As you write, focus on being clear, not clever. Focus on the ideas and information that you want other people to absorb. If your sentences have more secret staircases than a Victorian mansion, it's time to clean house.
● A metaphor can be your best friend or a backstabbing enemy. Use metaphors to clarify and illuminate concepts, not to create flowery prose.

My text is clear, but it's deadly dull.

● Generate intrigue by questioning assumptions. Make readers curious with phrases such as "*You may have learned in school that. . .*" or "*One of the biggest mistakes in our industry is. . .*"
● Introduce counter-arguments. Anticipate objections and address them.
● Imagine writing an FAQ for your product or idea. What will confuse a new user? Posing questions and then answering them keeps people interested.
● Read your text out loud and listen for repetition and clunky phrases. If you think you're boring, your audience will, too.
● When you are almost finished, make an outline of what you have done. For example, if you are producing a slide deck, write down the main headings. Are they parallel? Do they tell a clear story? Reworking the headings can help you restructure your material.

FIVE WAYS TO STRENGTHEN YOUR WRITING

Be concrete, not abstract.

ABSTRACT *The three little pigs built houses with a variety of construction materials.*

CONCRETE *The three little pigs built houses with straw, sticks, and bricks.*

Avoid passive voice.

PASSIVE *The first house was built with straw.*

ACTIVE *The pig built the first house with straw.*

Use strong verbs to tell a story.

WEAK *The wolf was in the driveway.*

STRONG *The wolf waited in the driveway.*

STRONG *The wolf paused in the driveway.*

STRONGER *The wolf smoked his last Marlboro in the driveway.*

Show, don't tell.

TELL (WEAK) *The big bad wolf liked to break things.*

SHOW (STRONG) *The wolf huffed and he puffed and he blew down most of the housing development.*

Avoid converting verbs into nouns.

NOUNS (WEAK) "innovation," "disruption," "participation"
Building with bricks instead of straw resulted in a disruption of the economy.

VERBS (STRONG) "innovate," "disrupt," "participate"
Building with bricks instead of straw disrupted the economy.

Banish filler. Get to the point.

FILLER (WEAK) "I believe that," "The truth is," "Like I said"
I believe that we should use bricks, not straw.

NO FILLER (STRONG) *We should use bricks, not straw.*

KILL YOUR DARLINGS Legendary American novelist William Faulkner helped make famous the phrase "Kill your darlings." Writers must learn to slash—without remorse—their most beloved passages of pampered prose. Be advised to wait a few days or weeks, however, before attempting this brutal work, as time emboldens the cold eye of the editor. The phrase "murder your darlings" orginated in a 1914 lecture by a now-forgotten writing professor. See Forrest Wickman, "Who Really Said You Should 'Kill Your Darlings'?" *Slate*, October 18, 2013, http://www.slate.com/blogs/browbeat/2013/10/18/_kill_your_darlings_writing_advice_what_writer_really_said_to_murder_your.html; accessed July 22, 2017. Illustration by Jennifer Tobias.

Project Generator

TELL SOME STORIES Use these prompts to inspire quick brainstorming sessions or in-depth portfolio pieces. Mix and match the methods to stretch your storytelling skills. Have fun and seek the unexpected!

PROMPT	TOPICS	TOOLS
RESOURCE SHARING Design a system for sharing products and services with friends and neighbors.	Dog walking Power tools Toys Internet service Babysitting Grocery shopping Car pooling	22 Narrative Arc 26 Hero's Journey 34 Storyboard 72 Emotional Journey 82 Co-creation 90 Persona
VISUAL INSTRUCTIONS In five steps, create non-verbal instructions for a process.	Scramble an egg Hang a picture Braid hair Apply a tattoo Check air in tire Kern type	22 Narrative Arc 34 Storyboard
SPATIAL PATH Design a floor plan for a spatial experience.	Exhibition of local history Animal shelter Hot chocolate cafe Gourmet hot dog bar Adult lemonade stand Airport security	22 Narrative Arc 26 Hero's Journey 72 Emotional Journey 90 Persona 104 Color and Emotion 142 Multisensory Design
SELF HELP Create a product helping people with different backgrounds and abilities achieve a goal.	Manage anxiety Exercise more Eat more vegetables Eat more candy Write haiku Make a five-year plan	72 Emotional Journey 82 Co-creation 90 Persona 100 Emoji 104 Color and Emotion 138 Behavioral Economics
THE FUTURE OF Imagine what a product or institution will be like in fifty years.	Books Breakfast Money Prison School	44 Scenario Planning 50 Design Fiction 90 Persona 132 Affordance
PROCESS DIAGRAM Design a diagram of a temporal process.	Breathing Life cycle of frog Credit card debt Rain Cell division	22 Narrative Arc 34 Storyboard 104 Color and Emotion 118 The Gaze 126 Gestalt Principles

NEIGHBORHOOD MAP
Create a map that features several types of information not usually found on maps.

Trees
Trash cans
Ashtrays, smoking areas
Storm drains
Bike racks
Accessible bathroom
Security cameras

26 Hero's Journey
72 Emotional Journey
126 Gestalt Principles

EMOTIONAL SPECTRUM
Create a grid of icons representing nine different feelings or emotions. Design this visual tool to include people who don't read or who have a language barrier.

Happiness
Anger
Fear
Hunger
Thirst
Physical pain
Mental pain
Vigilance
Grumpiness
Comfort
Optimism
Boredom
Loneliness
Isolation

82 Co-creation
90 Persona
100 Emoji
104 Color and Emotion
126 Gestalt Principles

PATTERN PLAY
Create a pattern with a repeating element. Add an element that is different and easy to find and one that is different but hard to find.

Circles
Squares
Plants
Letterforms
Stripes
Polka dots
Eyeballs
Footprints

104 Color and Emotion
126 Gestalt Principles

GENDER NEUTRAL
Create branding and package designs for a family of gender-neutral products.

Hair care
Underwear
Cologne
Razors
Makeup
Bathroom signs

82 Co-creation
90 Persona
142 Multisensory Design

NONVISUAL
Design a product that can be used by both sighted people and people who are blind or visually impaired.

Remote control
Toaster
Public transit ticket
Map
Money
Watch, clock

82 Co-creation
90 Persona
34 Storyboard
132 Affordance
142 Multisensory Design

COLOR CODE
Create a system of colors and shapes representing nonvisual sensations.

Jazz
Coffee or tea
Herbs and spices
Emergency alerts
Perfume
Softness/hardness

126 Gestalt Principles
142 Multisensory Design

TAKEAWAY

Storytelling Checklist

Use this checklist to amplify the action, emotion, and sensory impact of your work. Don't worry about answering every question. See where these prompts take you as your narrative skills expand.

ACTION

How does your project depict action?

Are people, objects, or design elements shown in a state of change or potential transformation?

Does your project deliver a call to action to users?

How does the user participate in your project? What will users do with your project?

Have you offered users a chance to embark on a journey? Is their path free or controlled?

Could your project affect someone's behavior? How might people respond to the work?

EMOTION

Does your project express a single dominant mood, or a mood that changes over time?

What moods and emotions might users experience as they engage with your work?

Where will users encounter high and low points of energy, emotion, or feeling?

Where are potential pain points? Where could there be rewards?

Have you used color or imagery to represent emotion or to convey symbolic content?

Have you had an opportunity to build empathy with potential users?

Have you included users in your process?

What is the personality of your project? How is that personality expressed?

SENSATION

What visual journeys does your project offer to viewers?

Have you used Gestalt principles to create clear groupings?

Have you engaged viewers in active, creative looking?

Will a user with a specific task in mind find what they are looking for?

Have you used design elements to invite action from users?

Have you engaged senses beyond vision (such as touch, sound, smell, or taste)?

Have you used color, texture, or form to amplify the nonvisual senses?

THE HERO'S JOURNEY

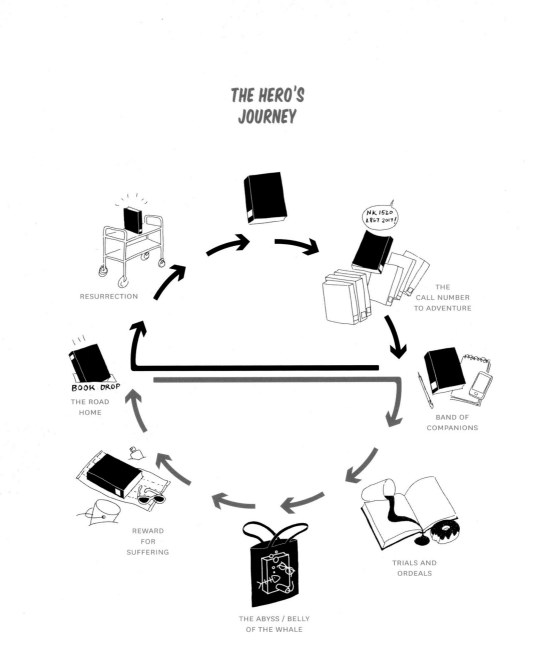

RESURRECTION

THE
CALL NUMBER
TO ADVENTURE

NK 1520
L867 2017!

BAND OF
COMPANIONS

THE ROAD
HOME

BOOK DROP

REWARD
FOR
SUFFERING

THE ABYSS / BELLY
OF THE WHALE

TRIALS AND
ORDEALS

Illustration by Jennifer Tobias